It's A Thin Line

By

Apostle James S. Prothro

It's A Thin Line

All scripture quotations in this book, except those noted otherwise, are from the Open Bible, King James Version, Thomas Nelson, Publisher and the Thompson Chain – Reference Bible, B.B. Kirkbride Bible Co.

Published by Robot Publishing Company
P.O. Box 961840, Riverdale, GA 30296
A division of JADOPRECRYS Enterprise

Cover design – Robot Publishing Company
Photography by Bob Johnson
First Printing – December 1999
Printed in the United States of America
ISBN 0-9662919-5-6

Table of Contents

Acknowledgement

I especially want to thank three ladies for their faithful devotion and dedication:

Rosalynn Curry, for her scrutable editorial assistance; Charmaine Johnson, for her constant and time consuming helpfulness in preparing my manuscript; Diaundra Coleman, for lending her hands to type relentlessly with a helpful heart.

Thank you ladies for your outstanding contributions. You are second to none.

Introduction

The story that you are about to read has been created, however it is indicative of many disturbing acts taking place in the body of Christ. Names have been omitted to protect all who are guilty, but please do not overlook the reality of the possibility of this scenario.

Here is the storyline:

The community is the body of Christ, consisting of a variety of new age, contemporary, pragmatic, secular humanistic churches where the people do what they want, wear what they want, and come and go as they choose. The church is represented by a club-type image. Like many churches, altars have been replaced with floral arrangements, covered monitors, and television strobe lights. Chaste and modest dress codes have lost out to the statement of "God doesn't care about what you wear." Mental massages and motivational professions, such as, "Money Cometh," have ousted rebukes, reproofs, and constructive admonishments. The phrase, "Money Cometh," is repeated until the concept is indoctrinated into one's mind. Offertory gestures and game play have replaced the experience of going to church and receiving a consecrated anointing from the Lord. Most sadly is the teaching that unrighteousness is automatically dispelled at the sound and growth of righteousness therefore, there is no need to mention the people's unrighteous ways. The perspective from which this book is written is not intended to include all churches, leaders, or their invited speakers.

Let's familiarize ourselves with the characters in the storyline and their roles. The pimp, the local pastor, enters his place of business, the church, and he notices the budget report sheet on his desk. This report emphasizes the need for more money. He whispers to himself, "We may have bitten off more than we can chew." Urgency fills the air. He mutters, "We must find more money quickly if our church is to maintain its status as a mega ministry." He sighs as he thinks to himself, "What would I do if I lost my social status? How would I face the public and my family if my membership dropped off and I was to lose fame, renownedness, and "my big-time preacher image?"

Unfortunately, too often this is the case in many of our churches. This kind of money pressure has changed the program from purity and pleasing the Lord to pragmatism and pleasing men. The pimp is forced to look over his list of speakers, surnamed prostitutes, he finds one that fits the description of the financial need of the church, one who is a crowd drawer, money getter. Let me emphasize that not all cases are applicable. It is vital that renownedness is considered while trying to determine who can draw the most people thus brings in the most money. A speaker is selected, contacted, and an inquiry is made about the honorarium (money given to the speaker for services rendered). In many cases, the honorarium is an astronomical amount and the receipts may amount to thousands of dollars. Although the honorarium may be a high amount to give the prostitute, it is justified because of the pimp's percentage that will be left on the table when the door has been closed and everyone is gone to their destinations with false hopes, based on a prophetic word from the prostitute. Let's not forget the fact that the scriptures used to give those prophetic words will often be used out of context and misconstrued.

The Board of Directors or Trustees Board may or may not be used in the decision-making for this type affair. Sometimes things are totally left to the pastor's discretion. This can be a mistake. Because of the game play that goes on among pastors in relation to the money that will be raised and the money that will be given to the speaker, greed and not God has become the motive. The parties agree on the basis of having already considered the count of the people, the number of offerings, plus the need to meet the budget requirements. If things go as planned there will be plenty of money left over for personal needs.

The down payment is sent, a contract is written and signed, and all of the arrangements are made and paid for by the pimp. He may secure limousine service, lodging at four or five star hotels, dinner arrangements at fancy and expensive restaurants, etc. Extra activities may include drugs, women, alcohol, or whatever special requests the prostitute may have when he arrives (not all cases are applicable). The prostitute may require this type of treatment or he may be a no-show. This is one sign that God was never in the plan. The cost is high for the pimp but the amount generated or collected makes it worthwhile. The pimp pays the expenses out of the church funds, which seldom is reimbursed to the church. He is assured of repayment, because he has already stroked the clientele by presenting a brief description of the prostitute.

Don't forget: the more renowned the prostitute, the greater the return from the people. The client, the congregation, is stroked by a brief description of the prostitute stating how anointed, prosperous, and what a godsend the speaker/ prostitute is. Emphasis is placed on how the prostitute started on a low level and how God has moved and blessed him in life. The pastor sets the date and time for the prostitute's performance and watches the clients respond, which makes him rub his hands together, lick his lips as if to say, "Mmmm good, money is coming to me."

Picture this in your mind, commercials, advertisements, and brochures are circulated all over town suggesting that there is an anointed event expected to take place. On the day of the event the pimp is elated at the sound of cars pulling in three hours early. Joy fills the air and reserved seats are roped off for special people. The prostitute arrives. The crowd stands to pay homage in expectation of a word from the Lord, a word on prosperity, a prophetic utterance about personal callings, etc. The pimp introduces the prostitute to the congregation. Remember, the prostitute has already stated his price to the pimp, and in many cases it is thousands of dollars, as stated earlier.

There are many pastors who are getting $20,000 - $30,000 for each speaking engagement. Sometimes down payments are made, other times contracts are written. The meeting time is set; the clients come and gather at the place called the church. Manipulation and motivation take place to influence the attitude of the people during what is sacrilegiously called the Praise and Worship Service.

After a period of time the pimp makes an announcement that the prostitute is prepared to start working. He gives certain orders. One orders is, "Don't touch the prostitute" another is, "Don't put your hands on him." The prostitute may have bodyguards to assure that these things happen. I am always concerned about the pastor who has bodyguards while teaching faith in God. The people are told that they cannot physically touch the pastor because he is so anointed.

The prostitute is introduced and he comes out and begins to "table dance" on the minds of the people. The clientele is mesmerized at the beauty and the eloquence of his speech. The prostitute's gestures often create a soothing and satisfying emotion. He offers prosperity, debt-free living, good credit comfort, and table dancing while the congregation begins to feel a desire to put money in his garter, in his hand, or they simply throw it on the altar.

Suddenly the speaker's preliminary act is over, he asks for an offering and the crowd's giving is manipulated based on what the prostitute has done while table dancing. The client, the church, in response to the offering appeal (to the chagrin of God) is also told that the offering given will "reap a harvest of many, many folds, more than was ever given. Some will receive thirtyfold, some sixtyfold, and some a hundredfold." When the client gives in the offering sometimes the prostitute will lay hands on each participant, as if to pray for them.

When everything is over the pimp counts the money received after paying the prostitute. In many cases, he is left with hundreds of thousands of dollars. The prostitute leaves, he gets in his limousine, goes to the airport, catches a plane to return home or to his next pimp. The client is left with a hope that is not based on the Word of God.

As ugly as this is, this is a clear picture of what happens in the institution sometimes referred to as church. This is also done under the pretense of crusades, conventions, seminars, revivals, and many other names, all of which propose to be God-oriented when in actuality it is all about money.

A THIN LINE

The line that separates opposites is so thin that it cannot be detected by the naked eye.

It cannot be fully known, clearly understood, and in some cases, detected by that which is natural.

Since it is not physical, tangible, nor material, it is safe to assume that it takes a spirit that is adept to the benefit or detriment of that **thin line** between good and evil.

By Apostle James S. Prothro

TRUTH, CAN YOU HANDLE IT?

According to the Webster's III New International Dictionary Unabridged and Seven Language Dictionary, *truth* is defined as the quality or state of being faithful; sincerity in character, action, and speech; genuineness in expressing feelings or beliefs; something that is the case. *Truth* is a general term ranging in meaning from a transcendent idea to an indication of conformity with fact and of avoidance of error, misrepresentation or falsehood. Truths are visions and insights apprehended by the whole man and not merely by the analyzing mind. Let us examine the word *truth* from the Greek understanding.

Truth #225 Aletheia; truth, as the Lexical Aids to the New Testament Book Aletheia; truth, is the unveiled reality lying at the basis of and agreeing with an appearance; the manifested, or the veritable essence of matter. The reality pertaining to an appearance. The adjective: alethes also means the same thing (Romans 1:18, 25) #227 Alethes; a true one who cannot lie. The one true God as distinguished from idols and all other false gods. Therefore, aletheia denotes the reality clearly lying before our eyes as opposite to a mere appearance, without reality. Used with three distinctive meanings: (1) Truth as opposite to falsehood, error or insincerity; Galatians 2:5,14; (2) Truth as opposite to types, emblems or shadows, St. John 4:23-24; (3) integrity, rectitude of nature, St. John 8:44.

For a moment, let us examine this very powerful yet misconstrued word, *truth*. We talk about it. We say that we want it. We are oh, so famous for quoting St. John 8:32, "And ye shall know the truth, and the truth shall make you free." However, if we were told the truth about something that made us uncomfortable or had probable incrimination, could we handle it, could we manage it, could we accept it, and could we allow its proper course in our lives?

Over the next few pages I will address the answer to this question and more. In order to express the truth, which is the purpose of this book, allow me to utilize the definition for the word veracity. While veracity is a synonym of truth, I would like to refer to it as the essential company of truth because it means devotion to the truth, the power of conveying or perceiving truth, and conformity to the truth. Most people are willing and prepared to accept what I will call "good truth." This is truth that is usually adorned with compliments and accolades, and gives credence to something that aids us or supports us. However, when we are challenged with what I call "bad truth," we tend to borrow from our human propensity of anger, as we get agitated at the idea that something would challenge our program. Usually, our programs/lives have the label of success, according to what we have defined success to be. When truth comes, it is often perceived as an intruder instead of a companion to help us improve and to make us free as Jesus states in St. John 8:32.

During the multitude of counseling which I have conducted over the years, I have sat in awe. At times, I have been discombobulated at how people shun the "truth" of a matter. Often I use the analogy of a tree when I am in a conquest between truth and lie as they sit on opposite sides of the counseling room. I look for the "root" of the situation and not the "branches." The branches can be many, and vary per every statement that is spoken. The root of the situation is often hidden under the dirt. Therefore, this book intends to dig up the roots of ministerial deception by unscrupulous leaders, money manipulation, and mind control; all of which lead to the spirit of common salvation and the influence of pragmatism which, I believe has actually destroyed the forest of spirituality that God intended for us.

In my analogy, notice, the roots are underneath the dirt. Our ulterior motives are often wrong perhaps causing us to have a period or tenure when we succeed at something that is not right, so much so that it becomes comfortable to us. This is what I call bad fruit, no matter how good it looks. The more we "succeed" without correcting it, regardless of what it is, the more dirt covers its root. While the branches are green and the buds show forth fruit, still the truth of the analogy is that the root of the problem is still underneath the dirt. People cannot really see the dirt because it is covered by green grass, which can easily be perceived as prosperity. So here is the picture. You look at a tree and you see the branches, the budding, the harbinger, the fruit, etc. Then you see the grass and everything looks good. Please, let us not forget that the grass covers the dirt that encompasses the root. We must get to the root of our problems if we are to stop a potential onslaught of bad fruit from entering our minds and spirits as God's people. We must start using the tool of truth.

Jesus makes it very plain in St. John 8:32, "And ye shall know the truth, and the truth shall make you free." I think that the word "make" is applicable here because of the struggles that we have when we are asked to do things via truth, which we really do not want to do. Sometimes there is a human effort on our behalf to strive against the Lord. Genesis 6:3 states, "The Lord will not always strive with man." The Lord is patient, merciful, and longsuffering but I think that there are times when the Lord's will is designed that He has had enough; His patience, mercy, and longsuffering put on brakes, and His wrath and anger accelerate.

I really believe that as we enter this 21st century, I have been given an assignment by God, which is not very popular to others or comfortable for myself. This assignment is to propagate a truth that challenges the character of many who are in leadership positions and have the "power of voice." I have lost my personality, yielded my character, and have surrendered to the will of robotism. While I still feel life in its abundance, there are times when I wish that I had not been assigned to the job that I have to do. This is a normal flesh feeling. In many cases the precepts of my teachings are not always accompanied and received with a desire for truth. Thus, I am misunderstood and taken to be "anti-us" when in actuality, I am just a little person with a voice that cries out in this wilderness of deception to "prepare ye the way of the Lord." I have confidence in the Jesus that I serve. He reminds me every day from Romans 8:31, "What shall we then say to these things? If God be for us, who can be against us?" He put me on a level that is not different from other men or higher than other men, but it is a level of clarity. I have a clear view of why it is so important that I speak the truth that is given to me. Please understand me when I say that I am on an assignment. This is not an assignment that I asked for rather, I was predestined and purposed for this assignment. God has given me the potential that equals this purpose. I am standing on God's promises and I have the power of God in my life. I have been able to write this book and others that you will hear about because of a passion to do what the Lord has told me to do. Most of all I have vision. In the Bible we read, "Where there is no vision, the people perish" (Proverbs 29:18).

It is often stated that Jesus was a radical. I am sometimes told that I too am a radical (one that advocates a decided and often extreme change from traditional views) and a rebel. While I do not believe that I am a rebel (May God, forgive me if I am because the word has a negative connotation), I do not think you are far off if you think or believe that I am a radical. However, the course that I travel must be understood as a desire to change "back" more than to change "from." While this may sound like an apology for what I am writing, it is more of an explanation of who I am. With this understanding you can then comprehend why I must write the things that God tells me to write.

I think that we have changed from what we, Christians, were and my calling is to try and help us to return to our first love as stated in Revelation 2:4, " Nevertheless I have somewhat against thee, because thou hast left thy first love." We have left it and we have entered into the gates of idolatry. We have forgotten about Calvary and its essence. We have totally forgotten about the promises of God for our lives. We have been mislead by occultic teachings that this place in which we now exist is Heaven, and that we should not have a hope of living in a place called Heaven in the hereafter (whether we go there or it comes to us is really not important).

In the book of Proverbs it reads, "Hope deferred (postponed) maketh the heart sick…"(Proverbs 13:12). I understand the pressures of our society: peer pressure, pressure to be like someone else, better than someone else, more successful than others, and pressures that come with trying to keep up. God did not intend for every man to be equal in what we define as prosperity and success.

California is a different size state than Rhode Island, but both of them have a similar system of rule consisting of governors, mayors, policemen, postmen, etc. So, the "size" of our calling does not matter as much as the quality we put toward maintaining the original essence of our calling, being stead-fast throughout our tenure. This book will serve to help us pull up the grass to get rid of the dirt and to put our eyes on the root of our lives. It may be that it is necessary to get rid of the part of us that is not "good root," faithfully trusting God for better character.

Regardless of how comfortable we are and how successful we have become at whom we have accepted ourselves to be, truth may compel us to change. Truth may compel some to stand before their church congregation and with discretion, apologize for teachings and beliefs that they have persuaded upon others' lives. Truth may evoke others to go to individuals and ask for forgiveness. While this book is not written to become a mandate in all of our lives, it is written to be a gift that sits on the shelf for every hungry soul who aspires to do the will of truth. It also serves to aid us in understanding exactly what we are vulnerable to and what we may have given into without realizing it. Some of the subjects in this book may be extremely difficult to understand because leaders have been blinded by the greed in their hearts. This book is not written that I may get some kind of selfish glory and human recognition. This book is being written because I have been assigned, as an angel of the Lord, to tell the truth in a society that is not given to hearing it. I have been given boldness without the fear of man. Man's facial expressions, his verbal threats, and his alienable practices are not enough to keep me from saying what "thus saith the Lord." Let us try to enjoy this book. Thank God He still has those who are willing to do the unique, peculiar, different, and the no-one-else-wants-to-touch-it type of ministry. God bless you and may His Spirit continue to multiply within you.

Your Apostle

A SPIRITUAL INVASION

"Beloved, when I gave all diligence to write unto you of the **common salvation**, it was needful for me to write unto you, and exhort you that ye should earnestly contend for the **faith** which was once delivered unto the saints. For there are certain men crept in unawares, who were before of old ordained to this condemnation, ungodly men turning the grace of our God into **lasciviousness**, and denying the only Lord God, and our Lord Jesus Christ" (Jude 3-4).

1. **Common** – Gk. (2839) **Koinos** defiled, common, unclean; to lie open to all; common or belonging to several or of which several are partakers.

2. **Salvation** – Gk. (4991) **Soteria**; from sozo (4982), to save. Deliverance, preservation, salvation. Used of spiritual and eternal deliverance sometimes used to refer to the perousia (the Second Coming of Christ): inclusive of all the blessings of Christ.

3. **Faith** – Gk. (4102) **Pistis**; from peitho (3982), to persuade. Being persuaded, faith, belief. In general it implies such a knowledge of, assent to, and confidence in certain divine truths, especially those of the gospel, as produces good works; miraculous faith or that faith in Christ to which, when the gospel was first propagated, was annexed the gift of working miracles, the doctrine of faith or of the gospel promising justification and salvation to a lively faith in Christ.

4. **Lasciviousness** – Gk. (766) **Aselgeia**; wontonness; readiness for all pleasure. Aselges, adj., is one who acknowledges no restraints, who does whatever his

caprice and unmanageable frowardness dictate. Syn.: asotia (810) wastefulness and riotous excess.

In the general epistle of Jude, verses 3 and 4, we find some very interesting, compelling and relative words. This scripture epitomizes the state of our generation. Jude addressed the destructive heresy of agnosticism, which seemed to have gained considerable momentum towards the end of the 1st century. This is similar to what I think pragmatism is now doing toward the beginning of this 21st century. It is gaining ground at a very rapid rate. A tremendous, tremendous change is taking place in the body of Christ. Jude addressed *common salvation.* I too think that common salvation needs attention, but first let us try to understand what pragmatism is and its relationship to common salvation.

Pragmatism is the notion that meaning or worth is determined by practical consequences. It is the cousin of utilitarianism, a doctrine that the useful is the good and that the determining consideration of right conduct should be the usefulness of its consequences. (Webster's Third New International Dictionary)

If a course of action has a desired effect, the pragmatist sees this as good. If it does not seem to work, it must be wrong. Pragmatism has its roots in governism and secular humanism. It is relativistic, rejecting the notion of absolute right and wrong, good and evil, and truth and error. Pragmatism ultimately defines truth as that which is useful, meaningful and helpful. Ideas that do not seem workable or relevant are rejected as thoughts. When we start using pragmatism to make judgments about right or wrong, or when it becomes a guiding philosophy of life, theology, and ministry, inevitably it is going to clash with the scriptures. Spiritual and biblical truths are not determined by testing what does and does not work because life, which is a definition, is usually subject to categorical desires. In other words, **if a desire for something is big enough and has enough people supporting it, then it can become the definition of what is right**. One may say that desire can influence definition.

Unspiritual, satanic, and demonic lies and deceptions can be quite effective and have become extremely prominent. In St. Matthew 24:24, we read about false Christs and false prophets that shall arise who will show great signs and wonders in so much that if it were possible, they would deceive the very elect. Majority reaction and agreement should not be the true test of validity. Prosperity is no measure of truthfulness. If we use pragmatism as a test of truth, we are supporting satanic methods. Pragmatism, if used as a guiding philosophy of ministry, is apparently flawed and dangerous. Nevertheless, there is an overwhelming, overpowering surge of ardent pragmatism that is sweeping through our evangelical ministry.

Traditional preaching and holiness teaching is being discarded or downplayed in favor of contemporary liberties. The new methods are supposedly more effective, that is they draw bigger crowds. I would like to emphasize again, as I have in almost everyone of my books, that **it is not how many we can count but, how many God can count on**. Attendance and numbers have become the chief criteria for gauging success for many of us. Therefore, whatever will draw the most people is defined as good and what we ought to be doing.

One of the most prominent signs of pragmatism is seen in the convulsive change that has just revolutionized the church's worship services in the last decade. Authentic praise and worship while doing what is sometimes called "breaking through to God" and touching the Lord has been exchanged for a more contemporary means of praise and worship. While we think that physical gestures such as the "Bankhead Bounce" (the name given to a secular style of dancing) and expressive movements with our bodies during worship such as would equal to the world's expression of worship using secular images, are cute, we fail to realize that this is a trick played by the enemy to increase pragmatism in the church. Some of our younger converts have brought their style, their system, and their practices over into worship and we have allowed it in the name of, "catching the fish before you clean it." This epitomizes the birth of pragmatism.

Those who formally danced on stage for the devil with various pop and rap artists are supposedly preaching the word of God. I watched a person on television break into the message about the Lord, go on stage, and start singing and dancing the same way he used to when in the world. As his feet started hammering the floor with rhythmic and erotic sequence, I knew in my spirit that this thing should not be. It was a mockery. The only difference between the spiritual and the secular was that a few words in the song had been changed to supposedly entertain young people. If we are not careful this can also deceive young people to think that anything is allowable in walking with the Lord. That is why this book is so important to us all and I feel such compassion for the people's need for the truth and a passion to write the truth.

These satanic influences may not stop. Christians must not cease efforting to stop these influences before we lose all hope for spiritual change. Do not allow yourself to take less than what God requires. Holiness is God's design for our lives. Truth is His vehicle to get us there. Let us take this train of truth and ride it to glory.

PROSTITUTION USING PSYCHOLOGICAL WARFARE

Psychological warfare has forever been a tool of Satan since the Garden of Eden. It was there that Eve was convinced that she was left out because of her lack of knowledge of the difference between good and evil. You would think that the knowledge of "good" alone would have been sufficient. The serpent made Eve think that the Lord God was hiding something from her. Therefore, he sublimely suggested to her that she should reconsider what was previously stated to her by God. What gave the devil the authority to contradict the Lord's direct, firm, and resolute statement? I believe that it was due to Eve's curiosity, her wondering, and her loss of focus. Knowledge was not an issue or a concern to Adam and Eve because they were doing alright strictly on the strength of their divine relationship with God. However, the serpent suggested (through the intercourse of psychological warfare) that they concern themselves with God's business.

There were plenty of trees to go around. In God's effort to protect man and perpetuate his life span, He instructed him not to eat of the tree of the knowledge of good and evil. The differentiating knowledge between good and evil was subordinate to the level of knowledge they were presently privy to. They had use of a knowledge that did not include sin, hurt, pain, frustrations, etc. The knowledge from the forbidden tree would introduce them to an opposite point of view therefore giving them options to choose from.

If we consider the formation of Adam and Eve from the dust of the ground then we would all concur that they did not have a chance with the knowledge that was available from the tree that produced the knowledge of good and evil. It would entice them to seek a type of knowledge that would ultimately destroy them. If the serpent was to be successful in his attempt to "defocalize" Eve then he would have to take away the idea and thought of "thou shalt surely die" (Genesis 2:17).

In Genesis 3:4, the serpent blatantly defied the Lord God's direct commandment to Adam and Eve by telling them, "...Ye shall not surely die." God said, "...thou shalt surely die." The serpent's response was, "Ye shall not surely die." The difference between the two statements is *shall* versus *shall not*. This nuance, although small, was powerful enough to cause a major problem and affect the total human race.

The serpent used mind manipulation to infect the human race, thus leaving us vulnerable to the venomous bite of psychological warfare. This war for the minds of God's people has been facilitated by the intrusion of pragmatic teachings and secular humanistic allowances.

We have added insult to injury because we have allowed our churches to be governed by leaders who engage in cliquish schemes that involve the promise of renownedness, prestige, and power. This trick is facilitated by the emergence of secular laws and teachings by behavioral psychologists. The vice of Christian victory can very easily be mass media and the transformation of American education. With this going on, how can a mind that is not stayed on Jesus expect to survive?

People are in jeopardy of losing their human qualities and freedom of mind through secret seductions if they do not stop and birth a consecration in the Lord that will afford them spiritual safety and security. This can easily happen by means of psychological, emotional, and intellectual manipulation, which is better known as *mind control*. The phrase itself seems so out of place for our Christian community. This can no longer be subject to a dilatory response.

One of my ministerial assignments is to speak a truth toward the position of leaders and pastors. This is not to make enemies. (Although the Bible says in Micah 7:6, "…a man's enemies are the men of his own house.") I believe that the strategy of ambiguity, with the intent to deceive while preaching, must stop. One of the ways to protect oneself from subconscious manipulation is to be aware of its reality and how it works to deceive the people of God. It has been proven that the subconscious acts upon what the conscious mind believes. It is similar to programming a computer. Information is fed into a computer and the computer responds to that information. If we consider the truth of the sad reality that many of our leaders and pastors are pimps instead of preachers, we can then start on our journey toward deliverance. Please do not forget that if the information fed into the computer (the mind) is wrong, it is still programmed to act upon it. If a person believes something that is not true, the memory of the subconscious does not capacitate the ability to correct the information but it does act on it.

If one desires correction from wrong teachings then he will have to seek the truth from a source that does not have an ulterior motive. Truth stands alone. It causes agitation when met with resistance. This agitation may be because of ignorance but most likely resistance stems from the fear of a threat. If our leaders have sold out to money and prosperity teachings out of perspective, then anyone or anything that threatens this program is called "the enemy." I have often been referred to as "anti-us." The theory of cognitive dissonance implies that the mind automatically and involuntarily rejects information that is not in line with previously accepted thoughts and beliefs. I believe this theory has become a law. Therefore, when the writings of this book reach your mind and your consciousness, it may appear as an attack against you. Actually, it is a life raft to catch you from the drowning effect of seed sowing, seed faith offering, and prosperity teachings that are totally out of perspective.

How can we know if we are manipulated, if we are so willing to take the leader's word without researching that word for ourselves? Many of us have discerned the arrogance of our leaders and are not willing to deal with possible confrontation. Let me remind you that this too is also a part of Satan's ploy against the Christian body. There is not supposed to be fear between the pastor and parishioner. If there is, we must discover why. It is very clear to me that there is a *thin line between prosperity and prostitution, preaching and pimping, con-artistry and consecration, anointing and anarchy, giving and gaming, and spiritual security and seed sowing.*

It is our individual responsibility to search for the truth and share it whenever possible. Wisdom is teaching that all men do not have the same appetite and few if any always eat. Much of what is believed is never questioned, especially if the information came from what we have accepted as a reliable source. It is sad to even think why some people believe what they believe. Some reasons given are failure to study for themselves, fear of losing friendships, laziness, and no defense for the opposite belief. If we would only study God's Word for ourselves then we would be rewarded for our sagacity to realize when we are being deceived. II Timothy 2:15, "Study to shew thyself approved unto God, a workman that needeth not to be ashamed, rightly dividing the word of truth."

In St. John 5:39, Jesus adds flavor to my concerns. Something that is not true can be believed if that information is carefully timed and presented by an accepted and respected authority, thus rendering the recipient vulnerable to various teachings and deceitful propaganda. The purpose of propaganda is to direct one's attention to certain facts. Human propensities and proclivities make for a good menu of these facts. Every man is capable of all things. Few are knowledgeable of this fact. Thus, we become sitting ducks without a breeze when we think that we are too smart to be deceived. One of my favorite phrases is, "Don't be deceived trying not to be deceived." If we would only read then we could defend ourselves from this deceptive ministry that is spreading throughout the land, which promises the people of God that they can get if they give.

Propaganda is information or ideas methodically spread to promote or injure a cause, group or nation. It is the doctrines or principles propagated by an organization or movement. To be effective, propaganda must constantly short circuit all conscious thinking and operate on the individual subconsciously. The principles behind the law of propaganda are similar to the principles of mind control, hypnotic suggestion, mental programming, distraction, and repetition.

Distraction focuses the attention of the conscious mind on one or more of the five senses. This is the design for stopping conscious thinking, thus producing a state of mind that is similar to daydreaming. It no longer amazes me how a person can appear slumberous during church service, sleep during the sermon and only remember the part that talked about money and/or prosperity. It is almost law that this person has already been programmed to believe that a man's life consists in the things he possesses and that gain is godliness (contrary to the truth in St. Luke 12:15 and I Timothy 6:5). While this is the furthest thing from the truth, it does describe how the mind can think if it is filled with the propaganda of prosperity teachings, which suggest giving to get and vanity over victory.

This section may appear to be outlandish and in some cases boring. That is exactly how the devil wants us to think. He wants the defense against his program to seem so complex and unusual that resistance will drop the ball and go home. Fortunately, I have no desire to accommodate him. My strongest desire is to please the Lord and in so doing I cannot be expected to please man, especially when he works to the chagrin of God and the pleasure of Satan. My focus is on the day when we stand before God. I want to hear Him say, "...Well done, thou good and faithful servant: thou hast been faithful over a few things, I will make thee ruler over many things..." (St. Matthew 25:21). There is no glory in being labeled "anti-us" because that is contrary to the truth. In God's eyes, a leader is no more important than a member of his congregation. Everyone is the same. A member may be vulnerable to the pastor and still not be subject to deception. If we all would just maintain a close walk with the Lord, our light will shine in the midst of darkness and our victory will be automatic.

SEED SOWING: A DECEPTIVE MINISTRY

It is wrong. It is error. It misconstrues the Word of God. It is misleading. It is injurious to the future prosperity of the people of God. It is Seed Sowing, Prosperity, Get Wealthy, Debt Free teachings that are erroneously taught in today's more contemporary churches. The following pages introduce my opinion, which supports the antithesis perspectives of these money-oriented ministries.

The ministry of "Seed Sowing," where the word *seed* is representative of the word *money* is a blatant contradiction of God's word. Contrary to popular opinion, if a preacher, teacher, evangelist, or a leader teaches on the subject of seed sowing and return, using *money* as the seed, then, he should afford the return that he himself promised, especially since Jesus did not promise the same.

In all the years of my studies of God's word, I have never found a scripture that supports the use of money as a seed. I realize that this is a very challenging statement and welcome any scriptural disapproval, thus I submit myself to correction if found to be in error. Jesus used the metaphor of seed sowing in perspective and in relation to fruits and vegetables while intending in some cases to suggest *soul winning* (Genesis 9:7; 17:6; 41:52; Romans 1:3, St. Luke 1:42). Please consider this book as an asset to your ministry and not as a personal attack. I pray that it will serve to be applicable in clearing up the erroneous teaching of seed sowing, faith seed sowing, and harvest prosperity teachings.

In today's society, it appears that the churches are getting larger, the pastors more lenient, and the people more contemporary. There is an invasion of pragmatic, secular humanistic teaching founded on an egotistical and competitive basis for who can have the largest church and the most members. As I write this book there are approximately 700 people on my local church roll. In addition to this, there are thousands who tune in to our television ministry. None of this matters, if the Lord is not pleased with the results of our efforts.

It is unfortunate that the contemporary church has chosen pragmatism using monetary contributions as its standard of teaching. The promissory of these teachings should afford the return that is promised to the people. These teachings are not consistent with scripture. This does not suggest that I advocate traditionalism, that too is error.

I have my own company. In my company there are those who have sown what would contemporarily be called a financial seed. (I use this phrase only for a point of continuity and relativity.) The company itself has promised a return on all investments. The company's resolutions, by-laws, and governing principles, make the company responsible for the return. It makes sense. A man steps outside of the Word of God and promises a return for the gesture of giving, using seed sowing as his basis. Then, it is only proper that he becomes responsible for the return on the people's money.

Allow me to clarify this point: A pastor asks 1,000 people to sow/plant a "seed faith offering" of $1,000.00 promising them a return in an expected harvest using the scripture, "...some an hundredfold, some sixtyfold, some thirtyfold" (St. Matthew 13:8). Be mindful that this is scripturally used out of context. Therefore, I feel justified in asking you to consider the social economical programmatics relative to this type teaching. It is my opinion that the pastor could take the $1,000,000.00 received and invest it into something with a higher return than the common market. **Remember that you can only reap what you sow, no more, no less.** In other words, if you "sow" $1,000.00 then $1,000.00 is all that you can reap, unless you are referring to fruits and vegetables. The process of multiplication is applicable here. If we refer sowing and reaping to money, then the process of multiplication will have to come from some type of investment prospectus. Fruit seeds are "invested" into the ground. We do not invest money into the ground. It would be impractical, sottish, and asinine. Thus, if we use the word *money* then we should refer to it as such and not as a *seed.*

Why is the word *seed* used when the word *money* is implied? When money gains interest, the interest will serve to be the reward better known and misinterpreted as the *harvest*. In the scriptures, the word harvest is only relative to the souls of men and fruits and vegetables. The abundance is that one person's $1,000.00 has nine hundred ninety-nine more $1,000.00 to add with it, which means the invested amount is greater and so is the profit. In other words, there is more interest per month on $1,000,000.00 than $1,000.00.

This, to me, is what should happen to the "seed sowing in good faith" ministries. The interest should go to the investor from the pecuniary investments. We should not be told to "wait on the Lord for our harvest," but rather "check out the bank statements." Look at our gain, our return. The church or organization still reaps the benefit of the initial investment. This principle is applicable when using money as a seed. Unfortunately, this will never happen because of the fear of loss and rapacious, predatory greed.

It is only fair to the people, if the ministry gains, then the ministry should afford the harvest promised. Instead, we are lead to believe that God is going to provide the return while the ministry spends what has been given to God. While this is not wrong, it is somewhat misleading. I believe we should call it the "giving of money for the responsibilities of the church." This removes the image of "give to get" and adds the flavor of "give out of a cheerful and liberal heart," knowing the responsibilities of the church and taking part in it (II Corinthians 9:7). This is God's way. (This is a picture of how the phrase "seed-sowing" and its principles may be applicable if one chooses to use it as a foundation for the ministry of giving.)

Another option regarding giving is to tell it just like Jesus told it. Give because God gave. Two things that He gave were His only begotten Son and eternal life (St. John 3:16). This is the reciprocity of our little giving, and I might add a very reasonable service (Romans 12:1). What is the worst thing that can happen if we remove the phrase "seed faith offering," while adding the phrase "Give responsibly to the needs of the ministry?"

Here is what I think will happen:

1) People will be free from the manipulation of "give to get."

2) The church will take back its character as a Christian society and not a money market. This is done by evoking pure giving, and not by profit-oriented giving.

3) Business will take a back seat and the church will regain total spirituality.

4) Money will be exposed as the vanity that it is.

5) Everyone will be responsible to the Lord God for himself.

6) The church will always have enough.

7) The pastor can maintain good character and integrity.

8) People will come to church for purity and not prosperity.
9) Membership will drop off, (sorry about that), but character will pick up.
10) Compromise will be ostracized.
11) Fellowship will be true.
12) Leaders who operate as pimps will be unemployed.
13) The prostitution of prosperity will diminish.
14) People will stop preparing themselves to believe that the church is a lottery line.

My effort in writing this book is not to suggest that I am the Deliverer of mankind but rather to obey the requirements of my assignment. Let us get started in understanding what this book is trying to say. Please consider these very important scriptures:

- St. Matthew 7:15-20
- Acts 20:29
- Isaiah 56:10-12

In verses 3 and 4 of the general epistle of Jude we read, "Beloved, when I gave all diligence to write unto you of the common salvation, it was needful for me to write unto you, and exhort you that ye should earnestly contend for the faith, which was once delivered unto the saints. For there are certain men crept in unawares, who were before of old ordained to this condemnation, ungodly men, turning the grace of our God into lasciviousness, and denying the only Lord God, and our Lord Jesus Christ."

Many pastors have abandoned the respect of an oath that should include conversation between a person's former pastor and their present pastor, if for no other reason than to get an understanding of why an individual left their last place of worship. Because of greed and self-gain, too many pastors are prepared to allow the exchange of membership without contacting the former pastor and validating the storyline. If a person has the time to sit with a pastor and talk about joining that pastor's ministry, then the time to call the former pastor is available also. The cycle of building a church off of another's foundation will not stop on its own (I Corinthians 3:10-11). We, the leaders, will have to stop it. We can do this by being loyal to our fellow pastors. We should do unto others, as we want to be done unto us. Remember, if righteousness is the issue the member should not fear counseling about the reason they wish to change the location of their membership. When they fear, be very careful of their motives and reasons.

Many pastors testify that, "...at first, there was no one but, me, and my few" then, because God blessed it, their ministry grew to hundreds and in some cases thousands. This is the average storyline. However, if the record is revealed, many of these "fast starts" happened by means of undermining other pastors. You will know this has taken place when people leave a church, go to a new church and there is no harmonious fellowship between the two churches; rather there is division because of a disloyalty between the pastors to at least converse. This is not always because the former pastor does not want to change from some kind of doctrinal error. Many times it is because the new pastor did not want to submit to the laws of loyalty. Youthfulness and deceitful, strategic games have started many new ministries that are now defined as "really growing" and "anointed."

Many leaders who are "so-called" successful started their ministries by undermining their former leader or pastor. The picture is very clear. They sat under the tutelage of someone they defined as a mentor. As they sat, they carnally planned in their minds and schemed to start their own ministry from an already established foundation. They talked to one member at a time, subtly and cleverly persuading each member to accept them as an equal to their leader. Here we find that emulation is the root of the problem. It does not take very much to divide a church if one has been given authority and power to speak unto the people. They gained opportunity to persuade and influence these people to deviate from their original way of believing (please read Numbers 16 about the spirit of Korah).

It concerns me when I hear that people are saying that "the Lord God" has sent inexperienced leaders out from structured churches that were good enough for them at one time. I'm afraid it may be a "god" that sent them. It seems as though someone or something tells them to start their own church. They are not told to stay and help the former church that they say is in a terrible predicament. Furthermore, they connive in secrecy to leave and take others with them. Why the secrecy? If given the chance, those being deceived would probably not leave their church to follow someone else who does not have the character to be open about their objective. I have heard some of the most cosmetically dressed up words being used in these scenarios. Words such as, "Church, the Lord has told me to start a ministry. I am not asking any of you to follow me but I am leaving my address in case you want to come." Many people will follow them because by nature, people are always looking for some reason to go against the men and women of God who have helped them when they could not help themselves. How quickly we forget the bridge that brought us over.

Many ministries have been established from someone else's ministry and people have been stolen away from their dedication to their God-given ministries. The thief is compassionate. He promises a new start somewhere else. If the individual has borrowed money from the church they are leaving, it is pleasant to their ears to hear that they now have a "clean slate." They are under a "don't pay what you owe the church" new start mentality.

New ministries are being birthed and surfacing on almost every corner. The story is always told in the form of this lie, "We began with one, two, or three people and now we have all of these members." That is generally not the case. The truth is there may have been some undermining done. People were coerced to leave their churches. They were told the sinful secrets about the pastor or leader. They were influenced to observe his mannerisms when he preached, to watch how he lived, and to listen for contradictions in what he said. The motive all along was to get the people to feel a need for change. It just so happened that there was a ministry available, how interesting, how convenient. The new pastor just happened to be a former member of the church that the people left. No man should build upon another's foundation (Romans 15:20). (All scenarios are not applicable.)

This has happened to many churches, so don't be surprised if a church surfaces one day starting with nothing and in just a few weeks there are hundreds of members; some of these new members may have left the pastor's former church or its affiliate organization. It is a plot. It is a plan. It is very subtle. God has not ordained this kind of behavior. It leaves us vulnerable to the teachings of common salvation and the seductions of pragmatism. You cannot start spiritually in the midst of wrong and error except in secular humanistic settings. One who did not leave in the right way cannot start right. I challenge those who are pastors, to correct your foundation if you have disrupted other people's ministries to start yours. You should repent and ask for forgiveness. People, especially young people, are very vulnerable and unstable. Remember those who are drawn from others can also be drawn from those who drew them.

In the book I have written, *Man, God's Robot* I make it very clear that youthfulness is not to be trusted. In this book, there is a section entitled "Slices from the Loaf of Wisdom" where you will find the phrase, "Youth is a continual intoxication. It is the fever of reason, the cold of common sense, the flu of fruition, the virus of virtue, the pimple of power, the rash of rationale, and the pneumonia of new life." So, to deceive a young person through undermining should not be considered a master feat. Inconsistency in church membership among young people is quite prominent. However, the repercussions will be tremendous to the deceiver because of the detriment it could possibly cause to the deceivee.

We can feel this heartfelt message in the book of Jude. He uses the phrase, "earnestly contend." It takes an earnest effort on the behalf of each individual Christian to make it through the onslaught of deception that is flowing through the land. The contemporary church has made common salvation and secular humanistic programmatic teachings so attractive. Often the use of dress-styles, music, ostentatious participation, and demonstrative gestures, which are perceived as an anointing, are used to trap the young and curious mind. These things can be, oh so attractive.

I knew there was trouble headed our way when suddenly new ideas of types of churches began springing up. Organizations gave themselves names such as Full Gospel, Word Church, Word of Faith, etc. All churches should be full of the gospel and definitely Word oriented. The new names and phrases may suggest extreme liberality and rebellion against traditional beliefs while advocating unsoundness and mollifying spirituality. It has become obvious that something is wrong. Anytime you are successful at changing the former, you will also have to change and introduce something new.

In my opinion, earnestness has been excluded. Very subtly, the message is being taught that you do not have to be earnest. All you have to do is participate in obeying what the speaker tells you to do. However, Jude reads that we should earnestly contend for the faith that was once delivered unto the saints (Jude 3). Jude must have seen the drifting away, the dissipation of spirituality, and the church losing her essence. If common salvation is to rule, it has to dilute that which was previously established as the principle for pleasing God. These new contemporary issues are not geared toward pleasing the Lord but rather toward pleasing self through self-gain, self-centeredness, and self-absorption due to what we call "prosperity."

To earnestly contend for the faith is to often remember the mindset and character it took for the "older" saints to survive. It takes the same things for us to make it: praying, fasting, and most of all an intimate relationship with the Lord. We cannot afford to hear of others reading and studying the Bible and fail to do the same for ourselves.

Yes, we are your pastors and your leaders, but you cannot trust us to have a Word from the Lord that is not diluted with our own perceptions and ideas, even though we want so desperately for that to not be the case. Still, we are humans and it behooves us, as individuals, to study our Bibles for ourselves and to ask ourselves certain questions: Am I satisfied with my personal relationship with the Lord? Do I still have a conviction for my wrongdoings? Why have I changed the way I feel about the way I dress? Why have I changed the way I reverence the institution called church? When did this happen?

Things are not as they were years ago when we were lead to Sunday school and church youth programs by our moms and dads. In those days there was no question as to whether we would or would not go to church. Today, the church's standard has been reduced through leaders coaxing the people. Individuals are told to come as you are. This means wear what you want. This is echoed by the words, "God doesn't care what you wear." I contradict that statement. He does care. The face of nakedness in the church ought to be exonerated. We should teach modesty and holiness, and not allow fashion shows, dress competitions, and sensuous and lascivious practices pertaining to our dress codes to be the focus of going to church.

The institution of church is not a place for dating. It is not the place to look for a husband or a wife. This too has sneaked into our mindsets via pragmatism and common salvation. The Bible speaks of certain men who crept in unawares who were before of old ordained to this condemnation, ungodly men who will actually turn the grace of God into lasciviousness and deny the Lord God and our Lord Jesus Christ (Jude 4).

I am so glad that the Bible writes in the fourth verse of Jude that this denial not only is relative to the Lord God but also to the Lord Jesus Christ. Unfortunately, the name of Jesus only has minimal space in this new era of teaching. His name is not used too often in this era of pragmatism and it is vaguely established in the minds of people as the **only** name given whereby we must be saved (Acts 4:10-12). In this era of teaching, we do not hear about Jesus and His teachings, taught above Old Testament covenant promises and that which supports the teachings of prosperity.

We must bring the name of Jesus back into our teachings. We must look, analyze, and prognosticate the teachings of Jesus. He was God manifested in the flesh (I Timothy 3:16). Certainly He knows what is best for us. He knows what we need to do and what we need not to do. He knows what is manageable and what is unmanageable. He knows what it takes to make it into His Father's presence.

Some of the things we are now experiencing via our teaching does not include Him. "Common salvation" cannot include Jesus because He is always dealing with truth and He always puts demands upon our lives for self-denial. St. Matthew 16:24 reads, "...If any man will come after me, let him deny himself, and take up his cross, and follow me." Denying oneself is not the foundation of the teaching in this contemporary, pragmatic, common salvation-type society. Acceptance of self is advocated. The realization of self-worth and self-interest is advocated and it is taught, very subtly, that when you get into self then you can get into others and God.

I do not believe that a man has the capability of understanding himself unless God's knowledge prevails. Thus, Jesus echoes that you must deny yourself (St. Matthew 16:24). Consider yourself dead if you want to gain life (Philippians 1:21). When we allow ourselves to die in Christ and let our concerns be that of pleasing and serving Him, He has promised that He will supply our need (Philippians 4:19). He has never failed nor does He lie. He will always do exactly what He says He will do.

If we are greedy for lasciviousness and have tasted of the money god, (which has become the desire of many) we are going to slowly but surely excommunicate Jesus from our lives. I am not disregarding the essence of the law because Jesus makes it very clear that He did not come to destroy the law but that through Him the law might be fulfilled (St. Matthew 5:17). Certainly the promises of Jesus, from Genesis to Revelation, are ours for the asking. However, they must be taught and understood in the perspective of their initial intent and not just to support some bogus lascivious teaching that is used to manipulate people to give for personal gain. Although it is a good strategy that works in the world, it is not acceptable in the church. If we all would just stop and look at what is going on, we would see nothing but strategy and network marketing.

Spirituality does not seem to be the primary issue anymore. It has become second interest to prosperity. That is why worship has been given a universal definition; whatever I define as worship is worship. The churches with large congregational sizes only worship with those who have large congregations, leaving the smaller churches to worship with the small churches. If a so-called, "big time preacher" is asked to come to a storefront church; he most likely will not accept the invitation. Of course there are reasons why he will not go. First of all, the host church cannot pay him enough. There are not enough seats for the people that will come. What is wrong with people standing on the outside of the church while he preaches the gospel? What is wrong with that? Absolutely nothing!

You see this world has set itself up for failure. If you are accustomed to preaching to three thousand people and you do that every time you preach, then you really have to be humble and saved to take an engagement where there are thirteen people (and I literally mean thirteen). I wanted the difference to be that wide because it happens every day, to the chagrin of God. Numbers should not matter.

In my ministry I preach to hundreds locally but thousands by way of television. Still, I have a heart for those who do not have the hundreds or the thousands. I accept invitations to churches where there are thirteen or twenty or thirty people. I preach the same to thirteen as I do to twelve hundred. To me, thirty is the same as three thousand because God is still in control of my life. I believe that as long as He is in control, I will not be caught up in these influences and persuasions that invite me to think that these conditions are not prosperous. Also, I do not believe that if you do not have a big building with an elegant interior design that God is not in it. That is not God's way of operating.

Jesus taught often while the people sat on the ground, the wind blowing in His eyes, trash getting in His eyes, and dirt getting on His face. In spite of it all, He spoke with compassion. He did not consider elegance essential to operating. As a matter of fact, He stated, "The foxes have holes, and the birds of the air have nests; but the Son of man hath not where to lay his head (St. Matthew 8:20; St. Luke 9:58). That does not sound like somebody who would receive a call to come down to Galilee of Judea for the purpose of preaching the gospel, and he would be concerned about how many people will be there and what the honorarium will be? While I understand the practice of honorariums and even advocate them, I will suggest to all that we should never allow an honorarium to be the entailing point for sharing the gospel. If the basis and the motive of the fellowship or the invitation for fellowship are pure and honest, then we should try to accommodate all men.

Unfortunately, in some cases, people who attend small churches may be embarrassed, ashamed, and no doubt made to feel inferior and out of God's will if they were to visit the "big" churches. They may not know how to perform the art of seed sowing. (I think this is error anyway.)

Another issue to be discussed is the assignment of seats in the church. The more renowned an individual is, the more prestigious he is. It is this same prestige that promotes favoritism. If a person is a celebrity or a movie star, then they are given a seat on the front row. Getting a camera shot of that individual is important because their very presence will draw people to the church. This is the teaching and practice of common salvation. This is politics. This is a true picture regardless of how uncomfortable it is for us to speak it. Seldom will you see a movie star or a professional athlete sitting in the back of the church if the leader knows that he is present. He is always asked to come to the front. I wonder why? Why isn't the wino asked to come towards the front? Could it be that his stench is a stronger detest than our love for his soul? It may be that he will cramp our style and he does not have much money to give.

Please hear me very, very clearly. Not only does the leader gain by asking the professional person to come to the front of the church while asking everyone else to get behind, but the professional person also feeds off this kind of egotistical mentality of wanting everyone to notice his presence, power, and authority. The choice is whether to please the professional person. Please bring him to the front but do it slowly so that the camera can film his approach. Many will please the professional person by making an announcement that he is there. Often, if he is not given a seat in the front then he will not be back. Well this is just too big of a chance to take. Why not accommodate all men? It is the most amazing thing I have ever seen in my life and it is happening now more and more. If we do not announce that Betty Sue, who is from the neighborhood and has thirteen children, no job, on welfare, no car and a torn pair of shoes, is at our church, then why should we announce that some professional athlete is attending our church? Our perspectives are totally out of order. This is done for self-gain and self-glory.

Many pastors and preachers have asked me to introduce them to certain professional athletes who are my friends. Why do they want to meet these people so desperately? Everyone seems to be desirous of being identified with those who are defined as successful. Why is a man successful because he has an athletic ability? That is not success. A man is not successful because he scores more points than others on the team and is rewarded with large sums of money for doing so. That is not success, but achievement. If a man does not have peace with Jesus he is not successful. He is deceived and fooled. Knowing the Lord and being able to come down to a level as Jesus did, to mix and mingle with those who are defined as lower class, is success. Success is not worrying about what people say when they see you hugging those who no one else will hug because they are dying from AIDS. Success is going into neighborhoods and sharing with young women and men, God's plan of salvation; this is done without the television cameras and the support of the mayor. Church, we have got to change. This thing has to stop. This thing has to get back to the place where Jesus called it to be.

I remember a pastor saying to me one time, "Oh, I don't have time for counseling, training, and all of that other stuff. I'm about that dollar." Is a pastor supposed to be like this? I'm about that dollar? This means that when you look over the crowd, you are counting the numbers and multiplying to see how many dollars you are going to ask for rather than discerning the needs of the people. It is sad to see what has happened to our churches and how corrupt the leaders have become. The church has become vulnerable to those who have an agenda and a budget and nothing will stop them from getting the number of dollars that they need to keep the program running. So, if it means calling in the renowned to draw the crowd and to manipulate the people for their money then "by George that is what we will do." This is what is happening my brothers and sisters, my readers, and my book club members. It is about money. It is about prestige. It is about keeping what you have. It is about buying what makes you look like you are somebody so that others can be attracted to you.

Plans to deceive the congregation are being made in the minds of many of our leaders everyday. How much money is needed is being discussed before the service starts. This is not supposed to be the case but unfortunately it is. The Lord never intended for church membership to be equated with an amount of money. Your next visit might mean another hundred dollars to the ministry. Please watch.

You can easily see what I am saying. First, sit in the church and enjoy the word of God, the praise and the worship. Everything seems to be going fine. Then the "bell rings." Now it is time for everybody to really participate in the service so the ministry changes course. It is time to give. The ultimate error of all, I believe, is when the money game is played (put a number on how many people should give how much money). For instance, the suggestion is made that two hundred people give twenty-five dollars, five hundred people give ten dollars and a thousand people give five dollars. It does not take a rocket scientist to figure out that the goal is set for fifteen thousand dollars. The strategy is manipulative.

There may be many people who will participate in this type of lottery.

I do not believe that we should accept someone saying to us that God said there are “x” number of people who will give “x” amount of dollars. I just do not think we should allow ourselves to be pimped like that. When leaders say that they have an anointing upon their lives to take up the offering, pray for them. The anointing of the Lord does not directly affiliate itself with money and giving. These are only sub-purposes of the anointing’s purpose. The anointing of God is far above this mediocre and trivial gesture that has become the granddaddy of the church. This practice is not supposed to be. Giving is supposed to be a cheerful gesture, in our behalf, that demonstrates good stewardship over what the Lord has placed in our hands to contribute and distribute toward the needful things of the church. If the Lord chooses for us to give “x” number of dollars, He will do so without the help of the manipulation games sometimes played.

I would think it proper for leaders to come out of their studies and address the congregation saying, “Our expenses require us to ask for fifteen thousand dollars. We need this amount. We need everyone to participate.” I would think that it may be alright to anticipate a count and if the amount received comes up short then request the difference. If the goal is still unmet, then let us conclude that this is one time we have come up short. This, in my opinion, is a better way to do it than to start numbering people, and having prayer lines that are labeled $10, $20, $30, $100, etc. Yes, this takes place. There are certain prayer lines for certain categories of giving. I know because I have experienced it myself.

Allow me to share my story:

One day, during a church service that I was attending, I was asked to pray for all of those who were in the twenty-dollar line. Someone else was asked to pray for those in the ten-dollar line and the five-dollar line. Needless to say, I did not pray. I did not think that I could really force myself to be so ignorant and unspiritual about something as important as prayer. When money becomes the means and the essence of a prayer, then I think I will be infiltrating my own character to participate in such. I have made many people mad in my refusal to participate in their money schemes.

If I am invited to preach at any church and they ask me to take up the offering, then I will often refer the offering ministry to the deacons. That is not my job neither my responsibility. If I am asked to preach or teach and the host really intends for me to "work the offering," then I think he will be disappointed. Maybe that is why some of my invitations have been cut off. The taking up of the offering is not the entails of my calling. I will do so when led by the Spirit, but not with any kind of scheme attached. My only request is to give as the Lord has given unto you. It works for me. God blesses the cheerful giver and not the manipulated, goaded, influenced, and persuaded giver.

Often, leaders are tempted to be unscrupulous and cynical because they have gotten themselves in irresponsible straits. They need money and they will go to any extent to get it. However, when they start playing with the souls of people, they have taken the wrong road to get what they need. Repentance is required upon their hearts. If your heart has been touched and your root called to the surface, then please start, at this very moment, to correct this error in your life that can ultimately contribute to the destruction of those who are a part of the Christian body.

There is a principle of common salvation that is going through the land. It is needful that we preach, teach, and write about it, and encourage the people to earnestly contend for the faith that was once delivered unto the saints because certain men have crept in unawares (Jude 3). Did you know that there are many pastors who are only concerned about lascivious practices?

In Proverbs, the thirtieth chapter, we find the words of Agur, the son of Jakeh, spoken to Ith'-i-el and Ucal. Agur speaks of a generation, which now exists, that curses their father, does not bless their mother, is pure in their own eyes and yet not washed from their filthiness, and have their eyelids lifted up. We are now living in that generation. May God help us to hold on until He comes.

I was asked the question, "How do you expect to survive in a community where you are perceived as "anti-us?" After thinking about it for a moment, I quickly answered, "Surviving in the community of perceptive minds that are based on self-centeredness and self-righteousness is not what I am trying to do. I have already survived. Satan's desire for my life is that I reject Jesus as my personal Savior. However, now that I have inherited eternal life in Jesus Christ, I am strengthened with confidence in knowing that if God is for me who can be against me? (Romans 8:31) Certainly, He's more than the whole world against me." Understanding divine assignment should never include others' opinions of what the Lord has given us as individuals to do.

It behooves us all to dissect our relationships with the Lord and to make sure that we are doing the things that the Lord has purposed us to do, our individual gift of giving Him the glory. We cannot afford to be directed by others' opinions of our lives.

SEED SOWING OR SPIRITUAL SECURITY

In my opinion, the next few chapters will exemplify the character of my writings. They will afford you a very thorough and indepth study on the subject of seed sowing. Also, I wish to disclose to you how the erroneous teachings surrounding seed sowing are robbing us of our spiritual security because the apologetics of this type teaching is weak and lacks substance. I am somewhat uncomfortable and definitely unpopular among pastors and leaders who do not intend to deal with true realities.

The promotion of giving money and calling it seed sowing is one of the most blatant acts of manipulation that I have seen in my nearly twenty-five years of ministry. Satan has gained ground, with this kind of error, in his attempt to rape the body of Christ of their spiritual security. I believe that this is one of the reasons that there is a thin line between what God gave us as a perpetual prosperous security and what many have allowed themselves to believe is the tool of God. This is really nothing but blatant manipulation on the behalf of one who takes advantage of another using money games.

I realize that we live in a critical era, one in which mankind is vulnerable to one another. We should not have to guard ourselves against material that is categorized as Christian oriented or tapes that are spiritual in image.

In these next chapters I will address issues that are relative to a book that I recently read entitled, *The Planted Seed, The Immutable Laws Of Sowing And Reaping*. Also I will be making references to excerpts from a tape entitled, *The Seasons Of Sowing And Reaping*. Both of these titles have been made public and distributed by renowned pastors.

These sources are being used as a representation of the extreme error being taught as it relates to seed sowing. It is my belief these resources only intend to manipulate the giving of money. Since my intent is not to harm or cast a bad image on anyone, I absolutely refuse to list any names regarding these resources.

I will begin by using excerpts from *The Planted Seed.* (Due to the length of this book's title, I will abbreviate the title in my references.) Beginning on page 35 we find these words, "You determine your own income, it can increase or decrease according to the seed you sow." This, in my opinion, is blatant misuse of the phrase *seed sow*. I believe that the increase of our income is determined by our work ethics, efficiency, conscientiousness, punctuality, and responsibility. Your income has absolutely nothing to do with the money you give to a ministry.

Later in this book in the chapter on "Game Versus Giving," I touched on some of the trickery used in the church. I would like to cite an example of this type trickery in order to make my next point.

Example: The devotional part of most church services usually takes place before the tithes and offering ministry. The steward will almost always have to make statements such as, "Now it is time to plant a seed-faith offering." Why is this statement necessary? Truth is essential to worshipping the Lord. When we take a dollar bill and call it a seed, we take away the truth factor. Money is not seed. The seed is the word of God (St. Luke 8:11). Further when we put numbers on free-giving to God; such as 100 people give me $100, 30 people give $75 etc. God's principles lose their immutability because people hear implementations that are contrary to the truth. In my opinion, the phrases *seed sowing* and *seed faith offerings* should never be used in the church.

From the book, *The Planted Seed,* pages 31 and 32, in the chapter entitled "God's seed for you," there are several statements that I consider quite erroneous. (I must make it clear that my writings are not to defame or slander the author of this book; I only desire to expose the error in the teachings it suggests). While reading the following, I would like for you to answer this question, "Why is the word *seed* used when the intended reference is money?" I will need your help in order to convey my message in this section.

Consider these statements:

1. The only way he (Satan) can win is if you hold onto your seed. Givers are releasing seeds that bruise his head. *(The Planted Seed)*

The only way he (Satan) can win is if you hold onto your money. Givers are releasing money that bruise his head. *(Prothro)*

2. This scripture refers to giving as a seed. (II Corinthians 9:10) *(The Planted Seed)*

This scripture refers to giving as money. (II Corinthians 9:10) *(Prothro)*

3. Whatever authority the enemy is exercising against a believer, in any area, it can be broken with a seed. *(The Planted Seed)*

Whatever authority the enemy is exercising against a believer, in any area, it can be broken with money. *(Prothro)*

4. The authority of the enemy in these areas needs to be bruised by the sowing of seeds into the Kingdom of God. *(The Planted Seed)*

   The authority of the enemy in these areas needs to be bruised by the sowing of money into the Kingdom of God. *(Prothro)*

5. Your seed breaks, bruises and crushes any authority he may be trying to exercise against you. *(The Planted Seed)*

   Your money breaks, bruises and crushes any authority he may be trying to exercise against you. *(Prothro)*

It is very obvious that the author intends to camouflage the true meaning of the word seed, according to the scriptures, in order to promote the continuation of rapacious, manipulative, downright deceitful seed sowing games.

The author writes from II Corinthians 9:10 (KJV) and then gives the translation from another bible translation. The trouble that I have with this part of the book is that it does not include the 12th verse; which clearly states that this verse context and intent is for the purpose of supplying the want of the saints. Not building larger building in the race of selfish and egotistical gain, paying the airplane note and pilot bill, limousines, five star hotels, $1,500.00 suits and shoes, expensive jewelry, family annual checks, putting money in real estate and personal accounts, living extremely extravagant eating at expensive hotels, joining in with politicians, and most of all hiding millions while asking hard working people for hundreds.

Why is the pastor's personal bank account larger than the church bank account and why are the church bills not being paid? How is this justified? Why is a small percentage of the church's money going to the benevolence fund? I didn't say amount, I said, "Percentage." I believe that every church ought to tithe to some form of outreach ministry and they should do more than just 10%. The church's account may be larger than the average church but the percentage contributed to outreach ministry could be smaller than that of the storefront church. Something is wrong with this picture.

Giving is a fruit of righteousness. It's right to give. It's God's virtue. Those who give cheerfully will always have. In the II Corinthians 9:10 we read these words, "Now he that ministereth seed to the sower both minister bread for your food, and multiply your seed sown, and increase the fruits of your righteousness." This cluster of words is defined in the Greek as ep-ee-khor-ayg-eh'o; to furnish besides, i.e. fully supply (fig) aids or contribute: add, minister (nourishment unto). The purpose throughout the bible for the kind of ministry expressed in II Corinthians 9:10 was so that distribution to the needy could be done. This was not for the purpose of fulfilling the needs of a budget, which hardly ever include the downtrodden and needy.

If leaders would take to the streets for the purpose of ministering to the homeless and go into the hospitals to visit the sick, if the poor could get the front row seats in the church, if counseling could be provided for the poor and needy from the pastors as easily as the rich and famous, maybe I could understand the low budget percentage.

We should not suggest a mollified meaning of the scriptures contingent upon our personal interpretations, which are usually based on us trying to justify our positions. The writer of *The Planted Seed* uses the words soweth, reap, sparingly, bountifully, and sown to refer to money. Money is an inference on the behalf author. The actual biblical reference is to vegetables and fruits. This scripture is about taking seed to the farmer who will do the farming for you. No doubt the farmer has the land and the know how to farm the land. His gains, profits, and percentages, from farming for you are great and your harvest will be also. You are helping him while you are helping yourself. This is a righteous act. The multiplication of your seed sown expresses the fact that if you have seed (vegetables and fruits) sitting in the house with no land to plant them, they are of no avail. Use someone else's land and both persons will win. This is the law of farming and not the law of giving or of seed sowing as it relates to money.

To use the word *seed* when meaning *money* is to rob vulnerable people of their freedom in giving while manipulating them to think that if they give more they can get more money. Money does not have within it the capacity to produce more of its kind; therefore it should not be used as a parallel to a seed or seed sowing. The thief does come (St. John 10:10) but spiritual leaders should not be thieves. St. John 10:1-10 suggests that the thieves be called hirelings, they come in through another door. They do not care about the sheep only about personal gain. They speak in undertones saying, "Ya'll help me pay my bills and feed my staff." Me, my and mine are the bags that hold the money.

Things did not have to come to the point of "robbing Peter to pay Paul." Detours on the way to the bank sometimes end in church money being placed in the personal bank accounts of spiritual leaders, and in some cases safes at home. I wish to write on this "travesty headed for tragedy" with truth that is as blatant as the erroneous teaching it opposes.

In Isaiah 56:10-12 we read, "His watchmen are blind: they are all ignorant, they are all dumb dogs, they cannot bark; sleeping, lying down, loving to slumber. Yea, they are greedy dogs which can never have enough, and they are shepherds that cannot understand: they all look to their own way, every one for his gain, from his quarter. Come ye, say they, I will fetch wine, and we will fill ourselves with strong drink; and to morrow shall be as this day, and much more abundant." This rebuke is much needed. These verses epitomize much of our church society as it relates to our leaders and the manipulation games that are being played. They love the idea of being called watchmen. Isaiah seems to have had foreknowledge about the present state of our contemporary church society. In considering the erroneous teachings of seed sowing as a means of prosperity, we must consider that this scriptural text gives us certain classifications of which we should be concerned.

First, the leader is blind. This could mean he is not illumined, or it could mean that the god of this world has blinded his mind so that he cannot believe, lest the light of the glorious gospel should shine on him (II Corinthians 4:4). The scripture continues in its admonishment by describing the watchman, the leader, as ignorant. The Bible concurs that we have the advantage and can only lose it if we are ignorant. "Lest Satan should get an advantage of us: for we are not ignorant of his devices" (II Corinthians 2:11). The Prophet goes on to say that the leaders and the watchmen are like dumb dogs, which cannot bark. If a dog does not bark, he cannot serve to warn those who he is protect. This scripture also describes this same group of leaders as loving slumber and taking comfort in laziness.

Regarding laziness I would like to ask a question, "Why are there so many revisions of the Bible and so many references being made to revised bibles?" I believe it is because many of our leaders have become lazy in studying the Word of God. Many have opted for getting their revelations from what I call the "microwave method." The microwave method is when leaders simply read someone else's interpretation of the scriptures, knowing that the congregation will not check for accuracy. That is all it takes. This is known as "**GETTING IT FROM SOMEONE ELSE.**"

RAPACIOUS DOGS

Rapacious – Taken by force: plundering; ravenous: greedy.

Let's go back to the issue of leaders referred to as greedy dogs. A greedy dog will go to any extent, even fighting, to make sure that he eats. He aims to get not only his portion but yours as well. A greedy dog does not concern himself with how much he eats or the nutritional value of the food. He just eats to satisfy the insatiable desire of his greed. The Bible refers to this group of men and women as covetous and ignorant shepherds. I am thinking that this may mean a loss of perspective. These greedy dogs, spiritual leaders are not as concerned about the souls of men and women as they are about the people's ability to give money to their institutions under the surname of *seed sowing*. I think these leaders may have been called ignorant shepherds through the word because they have been blinded by Satan to think that they can get away with erroneous teachings. This could be due to the multitude that flock behind them, complimenting their egotistical arrogance. In addition, the Bible also states that they are selfish and only consecrated for gain. Selfishness is a serious offense for a leader, especially when he is using others for his gain. This also includes those who surround the leader.

I advocate making the financial records of the church available to all members who pay tithes. Each and every person should be able to look at the church records to see how the money is being spent. We will not be so easily manipulated by those who we will eventually come to disrespect, and in some cases have ill-feelings toward, if we will only read the Bible and see what scriptures are being used to support the teachings that we are receiving. Reading and researching for oneself is one of my strongest advocations.

Many pastors become vulnerable to getting off track. Much pressure has been put on them to only teach and expound prosperity. Where does this pressure come from? It comes from leaders yielding their ears to the voice of the people instead of the voice of the Lord. This puts them under pressure to continue in error if they are to maintain the money flow and membership. This also leaves them in a very lazy state of mind, considering they only have to minister from one school of thought.

The seed sowing ministry that we have been flooded with, can be understood and seen very plainly and clearly as error. If only we would consider the Bible, the writings of this book, and other books that I have written, we will find that these teachings are contrary of God's Word. **Please be careful of anyone who may advise you not to buy, read, or study these writings. I am afraid that their purpose may be to hide the truth.** These writings are not to cause friction between leader and follower, but to give everyone the same opportunity to know the Lord with clarity and simplicity. Most of all, this book is designed to keep everyone from the entrapment of others based on gain and greed.

PEOPLE BEWARE OF WHAT YOU READ

When I first saw the front cover of the book *The Planted Seed* with the words, immutable laws, I became very, very concerned. God's Biblical laws are the only laws that are immutable. Laws, which have been birthed from someone's interpretation of a principle that justifies an ulterior motive, are not immutable. Someone's idea or acceptance of another's revision, especially when it supports what they believe, is not an immutable law. A belief based on doctrinal agreement is not an immutable law. I read this book to see what makes the laws of sowing and reaping immutable. My thought was, "were these laws the things that God has said and designed for His people."

Be careful of what you interpret as "God said." Many acclaim to having had the experience of God speaking to them. I am not sure if they mean that their "conscience familiar Lord" spoke to them, or if they actually mean that "God" spoke to them. I would prefer believing that they mean "the Lord" or "their spirit," as it is associated with the Spirit of God, revealed knowledge that God had already given to them. Thus, credit and credence is given to this knowledge as being from God. We must be very careful with this because sometimes credence is nothing more than interpretation. Misinterpretation is usually based on our already accepted and founded knowledge, which is sometimes based on our refusal to change and learn the true way of what we have acclaimed to be God's way. Misinterpretation misappropriated is how we get erroneous and deceptive doctrines.

I think we should notice how important it is when we start applying certain principles to our lives that suggest God's behavior. For instance, I believe that "God planted a seed in my spirit when I was saved" is a true statement if it means that we were saved with the Spirit of God. This Spirit is the seed of God that will eventually begin to develop as we enter into agreement with the Word of God for our lives. The seed is the Word of God (St. Luke 8:11). Human confirmation and in some cases affirmation, which is usually based and validated on our personal desires to see things happen, should not be classified as an angelic seed. It is probably better for us to believe that the Lord is using a person to speak affirmation into our lives while bringing us to the understanding that a seed was planted and is now being cultivated (agitated). The statement "God planted a seed in *my* spirit"(unless we are referring to the Word of God) is an erroneous and a very entrapping statement in relation to the Word of God. When the Lord placed His Spirit in us, He planted a seed in us. He does not plant a seed in *His* Spirit rather our soul/spirit. His Word/Spirit is the seed. All else develops and evolves from the inside of His Spirit.

It is senseless to believe that the Lord has an operating mode outside the direct line He uses with His Spirit. Let us examine this once more. The statement is "God planted a seed in my spirit." My opposition is that God plants a spirit, which is a seed, and allows that seed to develop. Now some may say that this is trivial and it is being too picky but the entrapment of this kind of error is so broad and we are so vulnerable, that we must be careful of the nuances of Satan. No one in the history of the Bible, except Jesus Christ, has been used by God to be a *seed planter*. The same can be said of a *seed sower* unless, of course, we have become sub-sowers and entities of the same practices and principles of sowing using the only thing there is to sow, the Word of God. Currency, money, and material tangibles are most definitely not to be used as a representation of a substance to sow as a seed whereby we will gain a harvest.

Now, I would like to shed light on the principle of decreeing. Please be prayerful that you hear what the Spirit is saying. Anyone who takes on the role or the job of decreeing something upon someone's life must be careful because this means they are assuming the responsibility of commanding or enjoining authoritatively another's life. This further means that the decree is setting or deciding to determine or order by authority another's life. While this practice is very common, I am not sure if the character it takes to convey this practice by the voice and through the will of God is always equal to the excitement about it being done. To receive a decree or to receive a word from someone puts others in a very susceptible and vulnerable position.

I remember hearing some years ago that one out of every three Christians you meet, would be either trying to share a word with someone or seeking a word from someone. In actuality it was not the word of God that they were sharing or seeking, but words that would confirm what people already wanted and had settled to hear.

I watch prayer line after prayer line and so-called prophetic ministries. The pastors always show the good, the positive stuff. Adulterers are given good sweet words from the pastors. Fornicators, lesbians, and homosexuals, all receive a good word from the Lord. I wonder if God overlooks our sins and tells us all of these prosperous and good things about life simply because someone feels that it is a practice of the ministry that must take place prior to asking an individual to do what is called sowing a seed into the ministry or unto themselves?

We should be extremely careful about words, especially words like immutable, decree, and prosperity, because there is such *a thin line between spiritual security and seed sowing.*

We could persuade people to think that their spiritual security is in practicing what is called sowing a seed and reaping a harvest.

I enjoy reading publications by other authors. In one particular book I was very glad to read the author's conversation about a revival that their church was in. He made the statement that the seed on the inside had matured and was about to bear fruit, and that they would become new people. He went on to say that he knew that they were being ushered into a different realm in God but he was not quite sure where they were headed. However, he did have the confidence that they did not want to miss this move of God. To me this is precise knowledge. I believe this is an accurate understanding of the way God works. The Spirit of God was on the inside of them and it had begun to grow. Their tenure had obviously been filled with church services, prayer, studying, and seeking God's face. The seed had been nurtured. The Spirit of God had been cultivated and fertilized no doubt by their conversation with the older Christians, and it had developed a fertilized mentality, a fertilized behavior and character personality, and so they began bearing fruit. They began feeling the newness of another level. They understood that God was ushering them to a new phase of development, to a different realm and to another level.

Even though we do not know the entails of our purpose, nor our next level, we do know that we are destined to reach that purpose. This is made very clear in predestination. Our purpose could change according to our dispensation. As long as we know that we do not want to miss God, then the errors of our youth, which is a continual intoxication, the fever of reason, the pneumonia of new life, the virus of virtue, the cold of common sense, and the flu of fruition, will not be enough to stop us (Excerpt from *Man, God's Robot).* I am glad to know this fact. This information is good information. It is the way, God's way. It is not a seed sowing concept trying to control God's spirit. It is the Spirit, which is a seed developing from within.

I desire to make sure that we understand that the seed is the Spirit of God/Word of God. It is referred to as the Word of God in the New Testament. It is the person of God in the flesh, Jesus Christ. This is the seed. If one is going to plant a seed, one has to plant that which is from the essence of Jesus, from His character, and from His nature; not from an interpretation that results in the enhancement of his life through self-gain, greed, and filthy lucre.

Much of what we get excited and emotional about is a manifestation from the seed that the Lord has placed on the inside of us. I thank God that I have been given a level of growth that encourages me in knowing that God does not speak in dark speeches (Numbers 12:8). Often, there is so much darkness in speech when there is what is called "prophetic lines." Prophetic lines are when the evangelist/prophet may speak of things that are general. For instance, "Someone in here has pain in his back or legs, someone is under the doctor's care, or something is wrong with you, I do not know what it is, but God wants to do something for you." These things are true in almost everyone's life. We as leaders need to seek God more intimately so that He can speak His exact and absolute words through us making us His agents.

As I continue with *The Planted Seed* in the chapter entitled "God's Seed for You" (pg. 27) I would like to reference the use of Galatians 6:7, "Be not deceived; God is not mocked: for whatsoever a man soweth, that shall he also reap." The author states, "We will now examine the reproduction of a planted seed in relationship to the process of sowing and reaping." You cannot plant a vegetable-type seed and reap currency/money. More critically you can't plant coin/dollars and reap any more coin/dollars from that process of sowing and reaping. Therefore, when referring to Galatians 6:7 we should only use this as a foundation for reference vegetable/ fruits. Money is not applicable, unless ofcourse we use this scripture to create a principle based on a doctrinal belief. This would be so easy to understand if this author and others would use the word money instead of seed. I became concerned because I am not sure if we can establish a relationship between the reproduction of a planted seed using the process of sowing and reaping. I do not want to sound confusing so let me explain my position.

Again, my position on seed sowing is *that God placed the only true seed, His Spirit, in our hearts*. As His seed grows, it produces the fruit of the Spirit. It expels ungodliness as we excel in godliness. It increases as we decrease (St. John 3:30). If we take this principle and teach it as a sub-principle for the process of sowing and reaping with a motive to encourage financial prosperity, which the seed/spirit of God has already completed for us in predestination, we are in error in our application of this knowledge. In His Word, God makes it clear that we will reap whatsoever we sow, no more, no less. This principle is taken out of perspective if it is used in the category of gain (money) and what we call tangible prosperity, unless of course, we are referring to the prosperity of farmlands and the abundance of fruit orchards. If we are not referring to these perspectives then we are going outside the perimeter of intent.

I think it is only appropriate for me to emphasize that the first part of this scripture says, "Be not deceived..."(Galatians 6:7). Many are being deceived while trying not to be deceived. This is taking place because we are not adopting the independent responsibility of reading the Bible for ourselves. Again, Galatians 6:7 reads, "Be not deceived; God is not mocked..." or God is not derided. The verb *mock* means to writhe the nostrils at one in scorn, to sneer at. It occurs frequently in the Septuagint, rendering different Hebrew words, which denote disdain. In Proverbs 1, mock means despise. In Proverbs 14 it means to laugh in derision. In St. Mark 10:34 and St. Luke 14 it means to scoff at. It is an effect; derision directed at God when we fail to meet His requirements of real piety and of practical obedience by rendering the presentation of lip professions and outward shows of religiosity. However, the derision will not last long. It cannot suppress "good." Whatever we may pretend or even fashion to believe in our hypocrisy, the eternal principles of divine government are sure to work out their accomplishments, not ours. Each day God is recording our human activities. Thus we should remember that retributory consequences are accruing each moment that we imagine wrongfully.

II Corinthians 9:6 reads, "But this I say, He which soweth sparingly shall reap also sparingly; and he which soweth bountifully shall reap also bountifully." The usage of this scripture is often applied to pecuniary or monetary gifts. This application used to possess a peculiar propriety, founded on the benefits of the giving of money, is in itself a dry and useless thing, and would be the means of affecting one's prosperity. This gives no liberty. It does not warrant our limiting the application of the Word to the bestowing of monetary gifts.

Interpretation is allowable by the Lord, however there are no revelations that are given by private interpretation that can be attributed to God (II Peter 1:20-21). Since we are allowed to interpret, we must be very careful what we construe as the exactness and the absoluteness of God's intent because we are limited in our interpretation of what God means in His divine application. We are also vulnerable because it is our propensity to take the fractions and fragments of something and become so excited that we will miss the wholeness and the conclusion of the same. II Corinthians 9:7 proves the wider application, which was the relationship between man and his giving unto the Lord as opposed to a harvest received in reaping and sowing. The quality of the harvest is determined by the quality of the seed sown. In the form of expression, the seed sown is "reciprocated," that is, every seed has its corresponding reward or punishment. In a similar manner, the Apostle Paul expresses himself in Ephesians 6:8, "Knowing that whatsoever good thing any man doeth, the same shall he receive of the Lord, whether he be bond or free."

These cited passages along with other Bible references appear to appoint a day of judgment for each individual action, with an award assigned to each action. This view is likewise presented by such utterances of Christ himself as seen in St. Matthew 10:42. On the other hand, in the passage from Galatians 6:8, the eternal life, and probably the "corruption" mentioned seem to point to the general award of life or of destruction, which each man shall receive upon review of his whole behavior.

LEADERS BEWARE OF WHAT YOU FEED

It behooves me at this time to remind all leaders, that we too will reap the reward of erroneous teachings such as teaching based on self-gain and selfish motives; teachings that control the giving of those that God has furnished with material substance that can be useable for our benefit. The Bible reads, "Be not deceived; God is not mocked: for whatsoever a man soweth, that shall he also reap." When leaders laugh and brag about how much money they raised, the ploys used to raise the money, how much they received in revival after implementing their give-to-get scheme, and how many honorariums they received from a particular engagement, then they are mocking God. When an offering is lifted with "x" amount of dollars in mind because the speaker will get fifty percent of what is raised, and when the effort to encourage more giving is based on the understanding of how much of the "more" the speaker will get, then leaders have turned their character into that of greedy dogs with the aspiration of filthy lucre.

Be very careful when you imply that Galatians 6:7 says reaping what you sow means monetary gifts and expressions of gold, silver, etc. Moreover, be careful to remind all that eternity is where the true reaping will take place. One of Satan's strategies to get people to believe in erroneous teachings, such as reaping monetary gifts due to giving, is to do what I call "spreading a sublime commercial." This is teaching or sharing a testimony that may include someone's expression of prosperity from seed sowing. For instance, a person may testify that he sowed $500 dollars to a ministry and the results were that his income tax check, which would have been held by the IRS, was released or that his car, which was going to be repossessed, was not repossessed.

These situational and fate blessings should not be used to support the Bible and the principles of God as they relate to giving. God knows how to take care of what belongs to Him without sublime commercials, which are designed to indicate that if I do what you have done then I will get what you have. That would be "bad seed sowing" and the retributions and repercussions would not be very comfortable for the one who hopes for the same results as testified by another.

In *The Planted Seed*, on page 28, there is a paragraph that reads, "You see, the strategy of Satan is to cast a negative light on preachers and evangelists in order to cause people to have reservations about giving. He paints a picture of dishonesty and distrust by using sources, especially the television media, to magnify the problems of one or two people. Satan attempts to create a negative perception of ministers in an effort to deceive us into thinking or strongly considering that all ministers are crooks." My position on this concept is very simple. We give too much credit to Satan. When we as leaders, shepherds, and watchmen paint a picture of dishonesty and distrust we should not attribute this to Satan doing something to us, but through us. We magnify this problem when we fail to apologize for our erroneous teachings such as, prophetic words (not given by God), seed sowing ministries, and placing emphasis on the necessity of every Christian possessing a gift called "tongues" to indicate the presence of the Holy Ghost in their lives. This is not an attempt on Satan's behalf to give negative perceptions. These are negatives that should be perceived as such, taken to the altar, and turned over to God. It is an effort to deceive the people of God into thinking that God's Word has been misconstrued from its original intent and now it is being interpreted in its true intent.

My, how blasphemous and sacrilegious these behaviors are. "Crooked ministers" is not necessarily a false statement. There are many ministers who are crooks and pimps, who have the church as the prostitute and the people of God as the clients. They sit in the pulpit and assume their ecclesiastical position, and they pimp using the church as a prostitute, asking the people to give towards the upbuilding of the kingdom of God, when they know that that is not where the money will be allocated. What have the people gained except a sublime commercialized mentality that the more they give the more they can receive?

A SLICE OF WISDOM

When we move in the dark we are vulnerable to being tripped by the thin line between good and evil.

By Apostle James S. Prothro

THE CHRISTIAN LOTTERY

What has been done to the people of God by teaching them to give so that they can get? Why isn't this teaching called the *lottery*? It is epitomized as such when we walk into the local convenient store and see a line of people "giving" or "playing" a dollar in the state lottery in hopes of reaping much more. You see if the ministry of seed sowing was well meaning, leaders would use the word "money" because that is what they are trying to say. Why not say, "Be not deceived. God is not mocked. Whatever sum of money a man sows, that sum of money will he reap." Now, if you listen to that phrase, you will see that using the word money will give you equality at best. Also, the use of the word *money* casts a shadow on the lottery/seed sowing teachings. Let us do it again. "Be not deceived. God is not mocked. Whatever sum of money a man sows, that sum of money will he reap." The message is very clear. If you sow $100 then you are only going to get $100. If you sowed $10 then you will only get $10. There is no jackpot! Let us do that one more time. "Be not deceived. God is not mocked. Whatever sum of money a man sows, that shall he also reap." You cannot get an elevation in gain when you use the word money. If this is the particle point, why not alleviate the word money and use the phrase reaping and sowing? We are being deceived and we need to see it.

In the book *The Planted Seed,* page 28, I read these words, "His (Satan) devious motive is to keep seeds from being planted, and with many, unfortunately he is successful." There are no seeds that we can plant aside from the Word of God. We need to clearly understand how the Word is relative to our prosperity using material and tangibles as gains. There is but one seed of the spirit, which is the Word of God. If the word or principle of seed sowing is used, it is relative to the word, fruits and vegetables, which are tangible. There are no scriptures that contradict or disprove this fact and truth.

Leaders are quick to apply what I call the "Job's friends strategy." They start telling people that the reason their harvest or ship has not come in is either because the individual's patience is not up to par or they have committed some kind of sin. Further they are quick to tell the congregants that they must look within and try to understand the things that concern their relationship with God and His promises. They are also told that they ought to search for spiritual and/or inward revelation. The next instruction to the congregation is to ask themselves what went wrong during the waiting period that kept the promise from being manifested. In other words, the people are led to believe that the problem took place during the waiting period. If this isn't enough, the people are told that they have a responsibility during their waiting period. It is the critical stage of prosperity. It is a pivotal time when things could go one way or another. Further, they are told that many lose out on what God has promised them because of an unawareness of the precautions that are necessary during the time of transition.

I was "knocked off my feet" to know that someone would teach that a human being has the responsibility thus dictatorship in the critical stage or the pivotal point of whether something will or will not happen. If the principle that preceded our human actions is "you reap what you sow," then it does not matter what the reactions or the actions are subsequent to sowing. We will still reap exactly what we sow because sowing is the condition for reaping according to the Word.

Sowing is not just putting a seed in the ground. It includes watering, fertilizing, cultivating, and sunshine. So, when people are told that they must use precautions during this pivotal time, this critical stage of transition, this teaching goes beyond the boundary of good common sense. I feel it necessary for me to convey this message again. If the principle is "sow and then you will reap," then the word sow includes fertilization, cultivation, sunshine, water, etc. All sowing is done before the reaping. To instruct that one's actions, beliefs, and patience subsequent to sowing indicate the potential abundance in reaping, is erroneous. I could understand this instruction if it were taught that our subsequent actions could cause unnecessary "worriation" because we are definitely going to reap. Telling people that they control their harvest by their actions after doing what is called "sowing" is incorrect. You see if we teach what sowing really is, very few people will be vulnerable to deceptive teachings.

Sowing includes much, much hard work and we are dealing with a contemporary society that does not want to work hard. That is why these "get-rich-quick schemes" are so attractive to people. That is why so many people are willing to reach into their pockets and give their substance (money) in the form of what is called seed sowing, expecting to get something for doing nothing. It costs nothing at all to reach into your pockets and give a "piece of money" in the offering. In predestination, God never designed it this way. Someone's interpretation has been handed down to gullible people, promising them rewards through the use of a couple of testimonies.

The state lottery uses the same strategy as the church, or is it that the church is using similar strategies as the state lottery. One hundred million people play one dollar generating one hundred million dollars. They give away twenty-five million of that one hundred million dollars leaving seventy-five million untouched. It is the twenty-five million that impresses the "one dollar giver" to think that he might win. If you sow a seed of "x" amount of dollars and you think that because you sow that seed you are going to reap a harvest of more than what you sowed, then you have been gamed and are playing the lottery. If we use seed sowing relative to vegetables and fruits, then we will see that we can sow one seed and reap one tree that produces many fruits that have many seeds. Thus, we will have reaped more in number than what we have sown. The quality of our sowing produces the quality of our return.

As simple as it sounds, this is the practical truth of our survival: If you sow one dollar then you are only going to get that one dollar back at best because money does not grow and multiply like fruits and vegetables. Please adopt a practice to at least study to see if the Word of God will concur with what I have written.

As I continued reading *The Planted Seed*, page 29, I became more and more disturbed. I ran across this sentence, "We must learn what to do while that seed (promise) is in its incubation period." What seed? Is the author referring to our monetary gestures? What seed is in its incubation period? The only period of incubation relative to seed is the Spirit of God placed within us serving to incubate our potential, the power of God in our lives, the promises of God, the fact that we are visionaries, the fact that we are purposed, and the fact that we are passionate. These may incubate inside the Spirit but the Spirit, which is the seed itself, does not have an incubation period. You see the Spirit was birthed when the Lord placed it in you. The Spirit started its growth then. To incubate the Spirit is to say that the Spirit can be incubated or the Spirit should be incubated. If you were to define the word incubation and relate it to the Spirit, you will see that incubation has no credence and no place in relation to the Spirit. Again, the Spirit does not incubate and the Spirit does not need incubation. The Spirit-filled Word of God is the only seed of God. All other seeds in the Bible are relative to vegetables and fruits, and eternal judgment and/or punishment.

It was amazing to me how I would run across things that were accurate and things that were truthful in the book *The Planted Seed*. On page 30, this particular sentence caught my eye, "Jesus, Himself, was a Seed sown into the world by the Father in order to destroy Satan." I thought this might have been a typo when I read "**a**" seed sown, because Jesus was "**the**" seed sown into the world by the Father in order to destroy Satan. I think we should be very careful about calling Jesus "**a**" seed sown versus "**the**" seed sown. He is "**the**" only seed that has been sown by God into the world to destroy Satan. All other seeds are sub-seeds of His essence.

Here is where we get ourselves in trouble. We think that an idea, a goal, or an aspiration for prosperity is a seed. These are not seeds. These are creative thoughts that we have birthed from the seed of God within us and thus we have become knowledgeable of the fact that we can have more, do more and accomplish more. God released "**the**" seed. The book says "**a**" seed. God released His son, Jesus Christ. Then the book reads, "This show us the power of seed planting." It does. It shows us the power of God mixed with the seed (Jesus), the Spirit of God, and the Word of God that God planted in our hearts. This has nothing to do with money. My point is to shield you from the idea, from the psychological warfare, and from the sublime commercialism that "seed" and "reap" have to do with money. They have nothing at all to do with money. These have to do with first, the Word of God, Jesus Christ himself, which is the seed;

secondly, fruits and vegetables as we will see indicated in most of the Old Testament scriptures. Again, I emphasize no money!

Further in the book, *The Planted Seed*, pages 30 & 31 I read something that I thought was crucial, "God then anoints that seed and destroys the work of the enemy. There is simply no way Satan can defeat a giver. This is why he fights us so hard in our giving." It goes on to read, "The only way he can win is if you hold onto your seed. Givers are releasing seeds that bruise his head." First of all, Satan has absolutely nothing to do with our prosperity. He cannot, under any circumstances, under any rule, or under any law, stop what God has started as it relates to receiving and prosperity. This is true in the spiritual, natural, and material sense. We cannot hold on to our seed unless we are calling our seed something that it is not. The seed is the Word of God (St. Luke 8:11). Imagine telling a human being that the only road to prosperity is by holding on to Jesus Christ. This is a precious statement to teach. However, if one teaches that the only way to "win" is by holding on to the memory and fact that a monetary seed was sown and a material harvest will be reaped, then error has been taught.

Earlier, I made reference to one of the most misconstrued scriptures in the New Testament, II Corinthians 9:10, "Now he that ministereth seed to the sower both minister bread for your food, and multiply your seed sown, and increase the fruits of your righteousness...." I will later take the time to explain this scripture so that we can understand the errors taught as they relate to seed sowing, which is a thin line between our spiritual security.

This generation is almost dependent upon seed sowing, thus they have forgotten that they are already spiritually secure and complete in Him who is the head of all principality and power (Colossians 2:10). It is very true that the Lord rewards the liberal soul. II Corinthians 9:10 may be read in one sentence, "The liberal soul shall be made fat," stated by F. W. Robinson. He elaborates this point by saying, "In the particular instance now before us, what are the rewards of liberality which St. Paul promises to the Corinthians? They are (1) the love of God (verse 7); (2) a spirit abounding to every good work (verses 8-10); (3) thanksgiving on their behalf (verses 11-13). This is a very noble harvest and it is totally spiritual.

When you give to God (sacrifice) and you know that what you have given is sacrificed, it is not to be received again, even in this world. If you give, expecting it back again, there is no sacrifice.

A FOUNTAIN

Once I saw myself as a fountain filled with substance
Awaiting someone else's need,
This would serve as the fulfillment of my purpose
And to help was my passionate creed.

Then the voices of low self-esteem
started saying this and they started saying that.
I started listening to scattered fragments and doubting
trifled scattered facts.

These vices automatically reduced my status
to that of a reservoir,
My very goals and aspirations
drifted to a land afar.

My potential was gathering in the boundary
of someone else's purpose for me,
Belief and confidence in myself
I could no longer see.

I'm so bored, so out of it
I am as a reservoir as opposed to a fountain.
I should be flowing
and not standing for showing.

I think I will put pressure on this dam
and break the walls of this prison,
so, I may be free to be me.

By Apostle James S. Prothro

CHARITY DOES NOT CHEAT

Charity – Provision of aid to the poor; Something given to help the needy; An act or feeling of benevolence; good will; affection.

Cheat – To deceive by trickery: swindle; mislead; to deprive by trickery: defraud; to elude.

Charity is not "speculating in the spiritual funds" or making a wise investment with payment of interest in time or in eternity! Rather, charity's rewards are (1) do right, God's recompense to you will be the power of doing more right, (2) give, God's reward to you will be the spirit of giving more, (3) a blessed spirit, for it is the spirit of God Himself, whose life is the blessedness of giving. Love and God will pay you with the capacity of more love, for love is heaven and love is the Lord within you. Human love is our best earthly treasure. It comes from the Lord to us that we may give it to others. The dearest and most precious relationships of human life are the rewards of them that can give. In the book of Job, we are reminded of how the good and gracious man, gets his reward in the love of the poor whom he seeks to bless (Job 29:11-17).

I think it is necessary for us revisit Galatians 6:7 again:

Paul spoke of the law of the spiritual harvest as it relates to the quantity of reward; so much sowing followed by so much reaping. However, there is another law as well that is to be unfolded from these Galatians writings. This law is that a seed multiply into many seeds. For instance, a grain of corn or wheat produces many grains. In some instances, hundreds of seeds can come from just one seed. Money does not multiply money through the tunnel of sowing; it does so through investment.

There is nothing in the vegetable kingdom that is on a stinted scale. God, in His omnipotence, touches a cloud of earth, via His design for that piece of property where wheat seeds are sown. In a few months stalks appear which subsequently are transformed into bread. That is not all of the surprises of God's creation. It is amazing to find that the ground has yielded far more than it has received. Thus, in the physical world, when the seed's yield becomes accumulative, it produces a vast surplus, which goes to feed those that are unable to work.

Nature teaches the lesson of super abundance and not abundance. God's design has within it enough to supply necessities, comforts and luxuries, meet artificial wants, compensate for impotence, idleness and dissipation, and allow for a waste that can scarcely be computed. The same is true in spiritual things. Productive power is immensely rewarded. Hence, we can believe that the fruits of righteousness will infinitely surpass the work done.

The abundance of the fruits of righteousness graciously influences the church, uniting all in closer fellowship by reason of a common interest in Christ Jesus. Furthermore, the church becomes bountiful, with no lack of seed for sowing, fruits of righteousness abound, and great liberty is upon the church, which causes thanksgiving to be given unto the Lord. This idea of thanksgiving fills a large space in Paul's mind. It becomes, "many thanksgivings." the Lord has placed the seed within us and the purpose of that seed is to give Him the glory. The Jesus in us produces our prosperity as we obey His will for our lives.

Throughout the course of these chapters I have made many references to *The Planted Seed*. I would like to draw another reference from page 31 of this book to further make a point. The sentence reads, "Whatever authority the enemy is exercising against the believer, in any area, it can be broken with a seed." If this means the Word of God then this statement is true. If this means a love offering or an offertory contribution then it is trickery. This statement was a concern of mine because following it were the words, "The authority of the enemy in these areas needs to be bruised by the sowing of seeds into the kingdom of God." The areas referred to were finances, marriages, bodies, children, and churches. Now, I was not sure what the message was supposed to imply. Initially, I inferred that it meant, when you sow a seed into the kingdom of God, it bruises the head of the enemy. As I read on I received a clearer understanding of the intent. The words written to explain the passage were, "Your giving overwhelms the enemy." (I have yet to understand how giving can be used as weaponry or arsenal against the enemy.) It is very evident that the writer intended to imply that giving represents the seed that breaks, bruises, and crushes any authority that the enemy tries to exercise against us. This is just not the case. This is not the Word of God's intention for our knowledge.

Scriptural references were given in *The Planted Seed*: "He that observeth the wind shall not sow; and he that regardeth the clouds shall not reap" (Ecclesiastes 11:4); "He that goeth forth and weepeth, bearing precious seed, shall doubtless come again with rejoicing, bringing his sheaves with him" (Psalms 126:6); "Give, and it shall be given unto you; good measure, pressed down, and shaken together, and running over, shall men give into your bosom. For with the same measure that ye mete withal it shall be measured to you again"(St. Luke 6:38). These scriptures, especially, St. Luke

6:38 have absolutely nothing to do with the seed sowing of a financial amount and the reaping of a harvest of the same nature, absolutely nothing! In order to understand these scriptures to have any connection or relevance to finances you must infer a meaning different from the original context in which they were written.

Let us examine the scripture from Ecclesiastes 11:4, "He that observeth the wind shall not sow; and he that regardeth the clouds shall not reap." The uncertainty and immutability of the future are not to make us supine or to crush all diligence and activity. He who wants to anticipate results, to foresee and provide against all contingencies, and to be his own providence, is like a farmer who is always looking for wind and weather, and misses the time for sowing in this needless caution. This scripture reflects no relativity to the seed sowing principle. Yes, it is used to indicate urgency without regard to what you may conclude as a cloud. For instance, finances that may be in trouble or in a bankruptcy status, or an eviction notice waiting at home, may be considered as a cloud. The theme for seed sowing ministry should be called "observing the wind and regarding the clouds." In my teachings, I warn everyone against giving a monetary offering with the expectation of getting a larger amount in return. That is not the way God operates. That is not what the Word suggests.

Psalm 126:6, is a scriptural text that further suggests the subtlety of some of the teachings that we have submitted ourselves to as it relates to seed sowing, reaping, and harvest. "He that goeth forth and weepeth, bearing precious seed, shall doubtless come again with rejoicing, bringing his sheaves with him." It is of my opinion that the book's author did not conduct detailed research to find the context of this particular verse. The picture that the author presents is of a discouraged man who had failures to the point of despair, he sows with tears and prays for no more failure. He sowed the only seed that he had. The Lord heard him and gave him an abundant increase. It is the authors suggestion from this scenario that you are to "give all you have," although you have tears in your eyes and things are not going your way. Give all that you have and watch what happens. You may have to weep tonight but you are going to have rejoicing if you give an offering. This understanding of the scripture is used totally out of context.

The use of St. Luke 6:38 to support seed sowing ministry is not unusual. The problem is that many have really gotten off track with understanding this one. Before we look into the thirty-eighth verse, I really am pressed to ask you to consider the writings of the thirty-ninth verse, "And he spake a parable unto them, Can the blind lead the blind? shall they not both fall into the ditch?" My first concern is that we remove the blindfolds from our minds regarding the Lord's will for our lives as it relates to our prosperity. Secondly, if we keep allowing our gullibility to trap us through trusting people's advice about giving, because they are renowned or because we have depended upon them to lead us to our spiritual security, then we will always be "short" and living beneath our privileges.

In the thirty-eighth verse it reads, "Give, and it shall be given unto you; good measure, pressed down, and shaken together, and running over, shall men give into your bosom. For with the same measure that ye mete withal it shall be measured to you again." The message is very clear that this scripture gives reference to the laws of responding to the act of giving, as it relates to our divine relationship with the Lord. It does not teach that you give and expect something in return, for then you would have lost the essence of the teaching. If and when you give, rest assured that your return will be no less than the original amount that was given, if your giving was pure in heart. It suggests that the generous giver will be the recipient of the regard, the gratitude, the affection, and when needed, the substantial kindness of those whom he has tried to serve. The prayers of the "good" may be added, whose worth is to be blessed, are calculable, or maybe even more valuable and more acceptable than any or all of these rewards.

The sixth chapter of St. Luke begins with a teaching on Jesus and the Sabbath followed by his choosing the twelve, the beatitudes, a lesson on loving your enemies, and a teaching on judging others. To amplify the detriment of judging others he uses what is found in the 37th verse. The first half of the verse, "Judge not, and ye shall not be judged:" is not the key part of the scripture or at least not more important than the second half, **"condemn not, and ye shall not be condemned.**" Jesus' lesson was clear and plain, if you judge others you will be judged. If you do not show love (verses 27-35) and mercy (verse 36) the same will be your reward of reciprocity. Thus we hear Him saying give love and mercy and you will receive these in good measure, pressed down, shaken together, and running over, shall men give into your bosom. This has nothing to do with money. Another way to explain this scripture is, the grand characteristic feature of the society of Jesus' followers must be generosity. They must be known as the givers of love and mercy instead if the judges of those who do not love or show mercy. They must have boundless generosity, unlimited kindness to all, Christians and non-Christians – that was the intent of Jesus' message.

Jesus' focus was not "give money and get it back." He enunciated to his followers that they must refrain from judging others. He uses parables to teach them what their ruin could be in judging; St. Luke 6:43-45 a tree is known by its fruit, and also St. Luke 6:46-49 the house built on a rock. We must beware of greed and self-gain. It leads to selfishness and the evils that come from loving money.

Selfishness often misses its own poor mark, and it always fails to bless its author with an inward blessing. On the other hand beneficence is always blessed. God rains down large benefits from above. Below, men offer their glad and free contribution. St. Luke 6:38 and many other scriptures, are often referred to as support for seed sowing principles when in actuality they support the credibility of God's response to giving out of purity and not giving via manipulation and con-games for the purpose of getting. That was not the Lord's intention for these scriptures.

Often, I am misunderstood and thought to be someone who rebels against others' teachings. On the contrary, this is far from being true. There were statements made in *The Planted Seed,* which demanded I express the opposing viewpoint in order to provide fairness to the reader. For instance, on page 33, there is a sentence in the book that reads, "It is important for you to realize that God cannot schedule your harvest until He has your seed." What seed? There are no seeds that you have that are separate from the fact of God. We do not own seeds. The sower went forth to sow. God supplies the seeds. These are God's seeds. If this statement were used in accordance with the scriptures it would indicate that God will not schedule your harvest until you release the Spirit of God that is in you back unto God. The word *seed* is misinterpreted if it means anything except the Spirit of God or the seed of the source, if the category is relative to fruits and vegetables. Thank God our giving does not dictate our return. Our obedience reveals our return within us and develops our prosperity for us.

The word sow is defined as to plant or scatter seed, to set something in motion, to impregnate with or as if with seed, and to put into a growing medium. If we consider these definitions, we will be knowledgeable of the truth of the sowing and reaping principles. It should be obvious that God did not put the responsibility of determining our own wealth or poverty upon us. If we think that our wealth is determined by planting seeds in someone else's yard we are mistaken.

Prepare yourself to stop at, what I call, "the station of revelation." God made us significant. We are His agents of glory. He uses us to please Himself. He protected our purpose by putting Himself in us to keep us in line when we stray, to help us out when we get in trouble, to encourage us during disappointing times, etc. Let us not forget that we are His responsibility in that we are His temples. "What? Know ye not that your body is the temple of the Holy Ghost which is in you, which ye have of God, and ye are not your own?" (I Corinthians 6:19) We must understand that we grow with Him from within ourselves. We develop as we study His Word and commune with Him in the Spirit. He is in us as a seed that is pulsating and prepared to evolve as a benefit unto us with access galore. We take the Word of God and feed it to our spirits through the rehearsal, quotation, declaration, profession, and most of all, the activation of the Word's character. This is called fertilizing the seed.

In our minds and hearts, we must agree that the Word of God promises the fertilization of the seed. Nothing changes this fact. This is a part of cultivating. God's credibility is not at risk and jeopardized by our human propensities, which are our inconsistent and weak ways as they relate to patience in our developmental states. Cultivation automatically induces participation/activation. The seed inside of us produces revelations. These revelations affirm God's promises to us and confirm our personal desires in relation to His promises.

I would like to direct your attention once again to II Corinthians 9:10 which states, "Now he that ministereth seed to the sower both minister bread for your food, and multiply your seed sown, and increase the fruits of your righteousness." How does this sound to you? We minister the Word of God to the Spirit of God which lives in us, by singing the Word, testifying the Word, quoting the Word, preaching the Word, etc. This ministry is exemplified most of all by living the Word as it convicts our lives. During this process, He that prepares tables of nutritious spiritual food for us in the presence of our enemies, most certainly accesses bread for us as our food. This is sort of like "if you scratch my back I will afford you eternal life." This scripture encourages our participation and activation in the process of reciprocity, thus the command to multiply and replenish from Genesis becomes a part of us. From this our spirituality will grow. This is called multiplying your seed sown.

Lastly, II Corinthians 9:10 addresses the subject of producing an increase from the fruit of your righteousness. When we are spiritual, for every moment of that compliment, we are constantly growing in the Spirit. (Do not fear confessing this for fear of arrogance.) God is big enough to keep us from catching up with Him and replacing Him. He can take all of our growth and more, and still be at the starting line.

III John 1:2 reads, "Beloved, I wish above all things that thou mayest prosper and be in health, even as thy soul prospereth." This scripture echoes my intent of conveyance. The soul's growth must be in parallel with all other prosperity. **The ultimate of all prosperity is the increase of**

the fruit of our righteousness, which is being more and more like God and growing in the Spirit.

THE MISUSE OF SCRIPTURE IS GROWING

II Timothy 3:16 reads, "All scripture is given by inspiration of God, and is profitable for doctrine, for reproof, for correction, for instruction in righteousness." This does not mean that everyone who has an idea should acclaim a revelation. There are no prophecies given from private interpretations (II Peter 1:20). It is scary to think that with all of the variations in revelations (one believing this and one believing that) there are no occasions where leaders are standing before the people confessing to wrong and erroneous teachings. Someone's wrong about this seed sowing game. I believe that it is a strategy for increased economics using hype and misconstruing the scriptures in the name of prosperity. My foundation for this statement is, there are no scriptures taught by Jesus that can be used to support these seed sowing prosperity teachings.

Many misuse St. Luke 6:38, "Give, and it shall be given unto you; good measure, pressed down, and shaken together, and running over, shall men give into your bosom. For with the same measure that ye mete withal it shall be measured to you again." If a person does not read for himself, he can be deceived to think that it implies the message of "give to get." It does not. Rather, it implies that if you give, you do not have to produce a selfish motive, desire, or responsibility. The fact is our gifts automatically induce the responsibility upon God's law of giving. The principle of this law is very simple, God knows what we have need of. He is not manipulated by our gestures because He is controlled by His credibility. In Proverbs 11:25 we read, "The liberal soul shall be made fat: and he that watereth shall be watered also himself." Proverbs 22:9 reads, "He that hath a bountiful eye shall be blessed; for he giveth of his bread to the poor."

When we "eye" other people's needs we please God, especially when we commit to praying for those needs and helping out wherever possible. These scriptures are all about giving with no expectation of a return.

Let us validate these teachings through Isaiah 58:10, "And if thou draw out thy soul to the hungry, and satisfy the afflicted soul; then shall thy light rise in obscurity, and thy darkness be as the noonday." God has windows in heaven, which contain a blessing that is too large for one person to receive. There are those who will give meat to His storehouse, which feeds others, and they are automatically recipients of these windows of blessing. God has chosen certain people for His principles and promises. They will obey God and He will support His Word. This happened in predestination and cannot be dictated by our present gestures. When we give, we should thank God for the opportunity to give and let that fact be enough to motivate us to do it again. Our motivation should not be based upon what we are promised to get. We cannot control our destiny by our present actions.

Think about this: If God did not know our present at the time when predestination started, then He could not have set eternal laws for they would have been subject to abrupt actions. What a chaotic world we would live in if we were allowed to set its tone by our choices. There is nothing that we can do and no amount that we can give that can change the fact that God has already given us a role in His video. Our actions are dictated by His choices, not ours.

There are many people whose hearts have been hardened and they will never be cheerful or liberal in giving. A non-liberal giver is a possessor of God's substance instead of a borrower. They operate off of the idea that "this is mine and not God's." This type of person usually demands a reward for what he gives or he will feel such a sense of possession that he will not give. At least this is what he thinks. In actuality, he is fulfilling a role to serve as the example of what is the opposite of good and proper. Every man has not been predestined to give good measure, pressed down, shaken together, and running over, thus it will not be given unto him for men to fill his bosom with gifts. This type person will always struggle financially, usually without realizing that this is the purposed predestined plan of God for his life. Or is it? Maybe this book will encourage someone to look at his heart, motive, and gestures, and see if they are pure and clean in the eyes of God. If not, take the Word of God and use it as the basis for change.

I Corinthians 13:9-12 (paraphrased) says, now we know in part, speaking of the present dispensation, but when that which is perfect is come, then that which is in part shall be done away. For now we see through a glass, darkly, but then face to face. Now, I know in part, but then shall I know even as also I am known. The Lord's knowledge preceded our actions thus our actions are subject to His knowledge. We are the subjects of His knowledge and the objects of His purpose. Therefore, it is already worked out. We only have to work with Him. Our efforts should only be geared toward praising Him and giving Him the glory. His promises indicate our success and prosperity if we keep these laws.

II Corinthians 9:6 states, "But this I say, He which soweth sparingly shall reap also sparingly; and he which soweth bountifully shall reap also bountifully." These are God's laws. They are already set. They are not capable of being manipulated. Not all men will sow sparingly but not all men will be given to obey the laws of giving. After man obeys the law to give, he will then have the categorical knowledge of his giving. This knowledge may or may not induce a change in mindset. If it does, and the change is for the better, then we can conclude that the role is positive and godly. The opposite operates the same. God has not trusted us to give, only to obey.

We have absolutely nothing to give. It all belongs to God. When we start giving to get, we have missed the picture unless of course, the man who suggests in his teachings that you will get from your giving serves as the bank and the harvest storehouse. This may work using the seed sowing principles. We do not need to help God with our prosperity. He does not ask nor solicit our help. He only wants our obedience.

In St. Luke, the twelfth chapter, Jesus particularly warned His disciples to beware of covetousness. He concerned Himself with their level of worry and anxiety about their welfare. In St. Luke 12:22, He tells them to take no thought for their lives, what they would eat, and what they would wear. He indicated that they should be appreciative for life and the body more then food and clothes. In St. Luke 12:24 we are asked, "Consider the ravens: for they neither sow nor reap," we, as humans, should learn a lesson from this, "which neither have storehouse nor barn; and God feedeth them: how much more are ye better than the fowls?" In the St. Luke 12:25 this question is, "And which of you with taking thought can add to his stature one cubit?" He adds in St. Luke 12:26, "If ye then be not able to do that thing which is least, why take ye thought for the rest?" St. Luke 12:27-28 asks, "Consider the lilies how they grow: they toil not, they spin not…. If then God so clothe the grass, which is today in the field, and tomorrow is cast into the oven; how much more will He clothe you…?" There seems to be an expression of a small amount of perturbation when Jesus says, "…O ye of little faith?

THE WORD HAS SOMETHING TO SAY

It seems to me that Jesus cares more about our trusting Him than our trying to manipulate Him through some plan of seed sowing. In St. Luke 12:29-30, He seems to convey my personal position. He asks that we not seek food and drink or be doubtful because of all these things. These things are what the world seeks after. In that we are different, Jesus tells us that our Father knoweth that we have need of these things. He told them in St. Luke 12:31 to seek the kingdom of God and all these things shall be added unto you. "For the kingdom of God is not meat and drink; but righteousness, and peace, and joy in the Holy Ghost" (Romans 14:17). Often I have heard this scripture used to imply that in all of the seeds sown, material things will be added unto you. This would be blatant error if one believed this interpretation.

Jesus emphasizes, in St. Luke 12:32, that we are not to fear as His little flock for it is God's good pleasure to give us the kingdom. I am really concerned about the conditions of our hearts, knowing that wherever our hearts are our treasures will be also (St. Luke 12:34). If I teach you to concentrate on earthly prosperity, then I would have robbed you of your spiritual prosperity benefit package. If we are God's then we are His responsibility and have no need to pay for His promises for our lives, which is often thought to be the case. When we learn to trust and obey Him, we will not be vulnerable to teachings that suggest if we do not plant a money seed we will not have a harvest.

We all can confidently state that God provided our harvest before we were born. We have to develop this harvest on the promises of God and as a purpose for our lives.

Thus far, I have referred to *The Planted Seed* and its contradictions to my belief. Therefore, I present my aspect on this subject of seed sowing because it gives clear opportunity to the seeker of knowledge to determine the truth for himself. Another area in which I disagree with the writings of this book, on page 34, is regarding the statement, "Success in your ministry, business or personal life does not just evolve; it is determined by the type of seeds you have sown within those areas. Your outcome or harvest will not and cannot exceed your input." These statements in my opinion are "fat lies" not "flat lies." They are overweight with error, obese in foundation, and therefore may seem unmovable. I intend to move them.

All that we will ever be we are right now, but we must evolve from God's purpose for our lives. That is the purpose of our potential. Every man that has ever done anything that is relative to growing stronger and getting better did so from God. It takes a capability and an ability to do so. There is evolution, especially when we use the substance of our potential. Our potential is the only true means of evolving. We are not connected to another human, but we are connected to God. Thus, God helps us to evolve based on His will for our lives. In other words He never made us to disappoint Him. He put in us what we will be and not what we are or would like to be. We do not have a choice. We have a role. You see, success is not your talent in forward motion; it is God's script in retrospect.

We cannot afford to think that a seed that is sown is the foundation for our success. If we were sowing these seeds to God as a condition that He has placed upon us, the author of *The Planted Seed* would no doubt have a point. However, we are not. To sow anything to God is to ask God to reveal, evolve, and develop the rest of Him in our lives. He will do this anyhow whether we do the seed-sowing thing or not. There is no man that has received less than what he has put in. We do not have enough to meet God's "wager."

I wish to further address the statement, "Your outcome or harvest will not and cannot exceed your input." This is found on page 34 in *The Planted Seed.* If this is an immutable law then how can it be manipulated? What have we done with predestination? This statement is a contradiction of the whole principle of predestination. If our outcome or harvest will not and cannot exceed our input, then there will never be any reason for me to believe in "abundance" as it is taught from these erroneous beliefs. It is consistent with Galatians 6:7, "Be not deceived; God is not mocked: for whatsoever a man soweth, that shall he also reap."

We only reap what we sow. I have heard it taught that we can receive a hundredfold in some cases. I have also heard about an increase, where our outcome will not and cannot exceed our input. May God help the mothers on welfare and the young couples that are newlyweds where both have jobs that do not equal "x" dollars per hour. There is not much left to sow after paying the rent, the car note, utilities, etc., especially when tithes are already given and offering shared.

I truly believe that if this scenario is your life, then God is not demanding that you plant a seed into a multi-million dollar ministry hoping for a harvest. The fruit of our harvest is our ability to think right and practical thoughts. For instance, we must learn to be content after we have obeyed the Lord. We must protect ourselves from the suggestion that gain is godliness; rather we should believe that godliness with contentment is great gain (I Timothy 6:6-10). What has happened and continues to happen at the expense of spiritual security is sad. Spiritual security is trusting God to take care of us without our help, only our obedience is required.

The law was written for transgressors, not you and I. If we obey God, we can say, "Okay, God." If we sow seeds it had better be into the Spirit of God where the harvest will be spiritual maturity and peace in Him. The Spirit only gives from itself what it is. Spirit gives spirit, not tangible and material things. Many faith and prosperity preachers should be challenged with this question, "When will my prosperity harvest come to pass?" The true answer is, it is already here as potential: our success, prosperity, and financial abundance. We must not forget that there are many sinners who have more material possessions than we have. It is God who puts prosperity in us to evolve from us. It evolves as we allow Him to work in us, planting a seed in fertile land. Our significance makes us fertile. We evolve from whose we are and not from what we are. When God is included in our potential, our potential and us develop into "potent." Always remember that He is God and we are because He is. God's timing and God's seasons do not need our input. He has predestined our spiritual security according to His need for our acts of glory.

Jesus states in St. John 11:4 the significance of Lazarus' scenario, "This sickness is not unto death, but for the glory of God, that the Son of God might be glorified thereby." In St. John 9:2-3 it reads, "And his disciples asked him, saying, Master, who did sin, this man, or his parents, that he was born blind? Jesus answered, Neither hath this man sinned, nor his parents: but that the works of God should be made manifest in him." My point is God manifests His results for His glory, not to prove His point and establish His credibility.

The teaching of a seed faith offering is a misleading method of prosperity. In His Word, God never promised to bless us according to our "giving" as much as He blesses our obedience to the laws of giving; then, we would have established our status of "blessed." When we release from ourselves (sharing alms), we not only release our substance but also the liability and responsibility of caring for what we had. This is why it is a blessing to have God's promises to take care of us. Our only responsibility should be that of pleasing God. His responsibility is to take care of those who please Him. Certainly there is no manipulation involved on His behalf.

I heard a renowned pastor, in the city of Atlanta, state that, "nothing will work for us as it relates to financial prosperity if we do not live a life of honor and integrity." Honor and integrity were given as prerequisites. A sinner and a worldly unconscious heathen can walk in honor and integrity, but who can walk in the Spirit? My point for this statement includes these principles. Most faith, prosperity, and seed sowing ministries do not allow the teaching of sin. The minister may "touch on it" every now and then but he will not dwell on it during the sermon. The big giver who lives in a common law marriage may be offended, the professional athlete who commits adultery may be insulted, and the homosexual politician may become angry. It takes more than honor and integrity to walk in spiritual security, which the Lord affords. However, these ministries are not about the Lord, but financial prosperity. Please believe me, we can use a Bible, teach from a pulpit, use scripture, teach on financial prosperity, and never touch spirituality.

Do not let the word *prosperity* fool you by equating it with spirituality. The world uses the word "prosperity" without spirituality. Unless it is taught as an Economics Class, I think that it is out of order to do so from the pulpit. Faith and prosperity ministries preach that every promise of God has been given due season. I agree. This is how I know that predestination prevails. After God's predestined appointment there are no disappointments. Those who God prospers He has given to obey Him. He has not given every man to prosper thus many men will not obey His principles.

Many leaders goad, evoke, and influence us to sow a seed. This may be the prosperity of the wicked. We must always consider our motives. The statement is often made, and I concur within reason, that "Expectation is not true expectation without preparation." This is very tricky. We are prone to think that preparation means getting ready for something that we are looking for. It also means preparing for what we already see. We are not preparing to see it, as is the case when we seed sow by faith. This eliminates expectations and the subject becomes a visible creation. In other words, it comes into view by faith and is formulated by fruition.

The promises of God make it clear to us whether the things we desire are ours. There is no need for a seed because it is already a fruit. The seed is in the fruit. The true principle could be a plant or a fruit instead of planting a seed. Jesus chose us to go forth and bring fruit (St. John 15:16). Again, He says in St. John 15:8, "Herein is my Father glorified, that ye bear much fruit; so shall ye be my disciples." God is glorified when we sow fruit more than when we sow seed. Seed is in the fruit. Then, the harvest is ready without the manipulation of seed sowing. There is therefore no need for planting.

Predestination seems to have done it again; answering question that most men fumble with. We all should give credence to predestination, for in it we find our prosperity, spirituality, and anointing. To think that there is a future day for us to get a return from a seed we sow is to be deceived. The day is already and has always been. I wonder if we will get a return from predestination's plan if we do not do what is called sow a seed? This is really serious. Think about it. We cannot believe in seed sowing and predestination at the same time.

"You've got to put faith pressure on some kind of expectation on the seed you plant," is a phrase used in a message preached by a renowned leader entitled, *The Seasons of Sowing and Reaping.* I will refrain from divulging the author of this message because it is not necessary. There is no such thing as "faith pressure." Faith is two things: substance and evidence (Hebrews 11:1). We eliminate expectation with substance and evidence and enter into jubilation knowing that God always keeps His promises.

If we are taught that there are nuances such as insects and bugs that destroy our seed planting, then we are being taught error. No one and nothing can stop what God started in predestination. The trouble with this kind of teaching is there is no way out once we start believing that it is in God's Word to plant a seed and expect a harvest, unless we are willing to let the truth free.

In Genesis 8:22, there is a popular verse used to support seed sowing. It reads, "While the earth remaineth, seedtime and harvest, and cold and heat, and summer and winter, and day and night shall not cease." This means Noah had prayer at the altar. God honored his prayer thus He removed the curse that He had placed on the ground (Genesis 3:17). Subsequent to His placement of a curse was His removal of the same. Ground that was once incapable of producing a harvest was made capable. This scripture refers to vegetables and fruits and not money as the seed and material gain as the harvest.

We have been misled. It is my opinion that God does not use this theology to keep His word. People who know the Word of God will not be deceived to think that they need to sow money to get what is already theirs. Do not forget that this may be just a fad. The very same scripture tells us of cold and heat, summer and winter, and day and night. This may be our hot, summer day but unless we have spiritual security (and not financial prosperity) we will reap cold, winter nights.

Please consider with me I Peter 1:4, "To an inheritance incorruptible, and undefiled, and that fadeth not away, reserved in heaven for you." It is clear that a gift has been given. It is great, precious, and promised. We are made partakers of His divine nature by this gift, spiritual security. We have also escaped the corruption of seed sowing and faith and prosperity ministry, which is out of perspective and has corrupted the minds of people, who at one time loved God, but now compromise with greed and gain.

The seed sown of all seeds is the Word of God /Spirit of God, which according to I John 2:25 has promised us, eternal life. There is no seed sown without the promise of harvest. This is the Lord's doing and not some artful work of manipulation by the pimps of our pulpits, using the church as the prostitute and the people of God as the clients. We do not have to adapt and operate in covetous laws. The Lord has a better way. Do not give to get. Get to give and then you will always have something to give and never have to worry about getting. Please be careful of the statement, "Let me teach you how it works." This may lead toward game and manipulation.

We are made to believe that there is seedtime and harvest time. My theology tells me that both of these are predestined times. However, for the sake of fairness I will ask this question, "Can anyone please tell the next man when is his harvest time?" Please do not depend on the preacher to share a revelatory word with you about what the Lord told him. This is just hype in most cases. I do not know of a scripture that indicates time for seed and time for harvest. It could be anytime. What happens if we seek harvest during seedtime and vice versa? There are so many loopholes in this kind of deceitful teaching for the purpose of self-gain and covetous rewards. Only the Lord knows the times of seed and harvest. I know that our monetary offerings are not the dictators of His knowledge.

Galatians 6:7 again reads, "Be not deceived; God is not mocked: for whatsoever a man soweth, that shall he also reap." I do not suggest that we amplify or revise too much of the Lord's Word for it may become a mollification whereby we placate our basis. This verse is not instructions for sowing into the life of the leader using the sixth verse as a basis for doing so. Galatians 6:6 reads, "Let him that is taught in the word communicate unto him that teacheth in all good things." The message in this verse does not mean to exempt the Galatians from the burden of supporting their teachers. Perhaps they were niggardly influenced in their giving and it was necessary to teach them their duty.

There was a time when ministers were teachers and not mere celebrants of ritualistic devotions or spectacles. They taught orally, as the word signified. The early disciples were "...nourished up in the words of faith and of good doctrine..." (I Timothy 4:6). The Word of God was their textbook. The early Christians were "...taught in the word..." (Galatians 6:6). They had the scriptures on their own tongues and were in a position to test the teachings of their guides as well as "to try the spirits." It is implied that the teachers preferred to devote themselves entirely to the work of the ministry. They isolated themselves from secular employment so why would it be necessary to provide them with an independent support? Galatians 6:6 teaches that ministers are to receive an adequate maintenance. They are to share “in all good things;” not as a gift or dole, but as a right; for Christ said, "The labourer is worthy of his hire.”

Luther suggested that, “Whosoever will not give the Lord God a penny gets his due when he is forced to give the devil a dollar.” Calvin suggested that, “It is one of the tricks of Satan to defraud godly ministers of support that the Church may be deprived of their services.” The Galatians were probably disposed to find excuses for avoiding the responsibility of supporting their religious teachers. The apostle warned them of the danger of self-deception and above all, the danger of imagining that a man may sow to the flesh and yet expect to reap the fruit of the Spirit. The principle of pastoral welfare somehow has gotten mixed up with the seed sowing/harvest principle. If the harvest refers to eternal life then we have missed the boat and fallen into deception.

There is a necessary connection between sowing and the reaping. It is impossible for men to break the Divine order established in the nature of things. There is a sowing time and there will be a reaping time. This is already God’s order and not man’s revelation from last night. Reaping is relative to sowing. He that sows wheat will reap wheat and he that sows cockle will reap cockle. Nobody expects to have a crop full of thistles after sowing wheat. If a man sows the seeds of charity, the harvest will be answerable both in kind and in degree. These are proper seed sowing principles because they are spiritual. The actions of this life are as seed sown for the life to come. The tare-sower cannot expect wheat, “for whatsoever a man soweth, that shall he also reap.” This establishes character and not amount.

The two sowings and the two reapings: "For he that soweth to his flesh shall of the flesh reap corruption; but he that soweth to the Spirit shall of the Spirit reap life everlasting" (Galatians 6:8). The flesh and the Spirit represent two fields where different kinds of seeds are sown. The future and the present stand in the strictest connection. The flesh is the unregenerate nature. Every act of life has a distinct relation to the gratification of that nature. The man who, "sows to the flesh," is he who "minds the things of the flesh," whose lifestyle is "after the flesh" (Romans 8:5), who "minds earthy things," who "fulfils the desires of the flesh and of the mind," and who "yields his members unto sin as instruments of unrighteousness" (Romans 6:13).

The terrible reaping: We see drunkenness dogged by disease, idleness with rags, pride with scorn, and the rejection of God by the belief of a lie. The passages found in II Peter 2:12 and I Corinthians 3:17 clearly point to the harvest at the end of the world, when the seed germinates into corruption. This is moral death. "To be carnally minded is death." Great in consequence will be the misery of man upon himself. All the acts of the believer have relation to the life of grace: he lays up treasures in heaven. The life created by the Spirit can have no pause; it renounces self and lives for God. The harvest is everlasting life, which is not material and tangible.

The harvest is everlasting life to all who sow to the Spirit. For the rest, "…every one may receive the things done in his body, according to that he hath done, whether it be good or bad" (II Corinthians 5:10). This passage suggests that we must have due consideration of the importance of our present conduct, and that the hypocrite is a fool who imagines that he can sow to the flesh and yet reap "life everlasting." It is only by faith in Jesus Christ that we shall ever be brought to cease sowing to the flesh and begin sowing to the Spirit. To sow to the flesh is to believe that money is a seed, which will eventually reap corruption.

If one wants to buy his teacher or instructor a Rolls Royce, it is allowable by the Lord and I am also sure it would be acceptable by the teacher. Thinking that one can give money as a seed and reap a harvest while calling it a return, without being in error, is unacceptable to the Lord's teachings and should not be. The purchase of a car is not a seed sown although it is taught as such. It is a gesture led by the Lord to be done usually for two reasons: the Lord has designed it for the instructor and the Lord has designed it for the giver. No other reasons are necessary. Nothing is gained by obeying the Lord except that which has been assigned in predestination.

We are often erroneously taught that when we submit to someone we can inherit their anointing. I am sure that this idea was derived from the Elijah/Elisha scenario, which was not an inherited anointing, more so, it was an impartation. Please do not be deceived, the only one from whom one can inherit an anointing is Jesus. It cannot come from your pastor because he does not own an anointing that can be inherited. Submission does not give us the right to inherit anything from someone else. It has to be in God's will. Many of the disciples were submitted but never inherited Jesus' anointing.

Every man does not have a seed to plant. Should he not eat? Should those who have, share with those who have not? The answer is obvious. The prisoner, the convalescence resident, or a citizen of a third world country may not have a seed to plant. How do we explain the professional boxer who hardly goes to church having millions, and his neighbor who goes to church every day is barely making it? Does seed sowing answer this question? Of course it does not, at least not without prejudice and bias. God has determined our prosperity. Our concentration should be on Him and giving Him the glory and not on our gain. Why don't we call the seed what we are implying, *money*? Money has only one letter more than seed. It is a common word. Why do we disguise it and hide it behind the word seed? The Bible tell us that whatever a man soweth that and only that, will he reap. How then, do we explain the concept of "increase?"

We can only reap what we sow. This is clear because it refers to character and not amount. We are quick to say God said it and we believe it. If that were really the case, we would not need to think about planting a seed and expecting a harvest. Notice that there is not one scripture where God or Jesus tells us to plant a seed and we will reap a harvest. This is what the preacher says from what he inferred. My concern is why didn't Jesus think enough of this principle to teach it? He did not and would not because the principle from which it is taught is wrong. He knew that His Word was the seed and the exchange of that Word from the Bible to our hearts is recognized as the planting, with spiritual growth as the harvest to follow.

I am going to close this chapter by taking one last excerpts from *The Planted Seed*. On page 38 it instructs us to, "be sure the soil is free of rocks and stones because the soil is symbolic of our hearts. If there are rocks and stones in the soil (heart), they will eventually gravitate toward our seed. They will press themselves against it, preventing its roots from developing, and destroying the roots that have already sprouted." I do not agree with this confused exposition. In this paragraph you will see the seed operating in two different places, the place where you plant it and the place where your heart (soil) is. Now if the soil is relative to the seed, and under a normal setting it would be, then the seed cannot grow without the soil. This is unless this writing means for one to sow a seed in a different place than just faith seed sowing ministry. If we plant a seed it had better be in the Spirit where stones and rocks do not work to our detriment. I suggest that we plant/sow seeds in the Spirit so that we will keep the harvest of eternal life. This is done through our sharing the Lord's word with those who are without it.

A stockbroker is aware that he has to invest a larger amount in order to receive a larger return. This return will still not exceed its promised amount, apples being apples and oranges being oranges. We reap what we sow. It is time to release our faith. Faith is not our money.

PROSPERITY OR PROSTITUTION

Prosperity is a state of healthy growth. In the definition section of the dictionary, prosperity is a state of high general economic activity marked by relatively full employment, increasing use of resources, and a high level of investment. This is what I believe is the basis for seed sowing/faith offering teachings.

Something just struck my attention. Prosperity is a major benefit of God's will for mankind. It is a condition of success. I really believe that prosperity reaches its abundance status when the knowledge that our prosperity is God's already predestined assigned responsibility, is added to our understanding. There is no work or effort required on man's behalf for God to do what He has predestined. In other words, there are those who will be prosperous and those who will not. This is signified in the poverty scenario of our third world countries. America should be glad that God has predestined her prosperity. It is an honor to live in the United States of America.

Our country was once based on the Word and will of God. When we took the responsibility for our prosperity out of God's hands, and started diluting His principles and contaminating His intent, we destroyed America's future without realizing it. Now we have two classes of people: those who have and those who have not. God's desire is for us all to have. Today's ministers have taken His promise of life in abundance and turned it into material and tangible possessions. St. Luke 12:15 says, "...for a man's life consisteth not in the abundance of the things which he possesseth." He meant life and life alone. Nothing else. Please study this scripture. It means life eternally. Again St. Matthew 6:33, "But seek ye first the kingdom of God, and his righteousness; and all these things shall be added unto you," and man turns this into an addition of material things. It means the things spoken of in verse 31, food, drink, and clothing. In St. Luke 6:38 we hear a message of justice rather than prosperity. We may infer prosperity from what we read because of personal desires. These scriptures are not referring to giving in the offering.

There are many, many more scriptures that have been misconstrued that need to be addressed. God does not need our help with His plan for our prosperity. He made and created those who will obey His principles and those who will not. We have become myopic in understanding these truths. May I remind you that the Lord hardened the heart of Pharaoh and created Judas as a devil, the son of perdition. It would not have mattered if Pharaoh wanted to let the people go. He could not because the Lord's intent was to show His delivering power through the obedience of the children of Israel. Pharaoh had a job to do and he did it well. He had a role to play and he played it well.

Our prosperity is God's responsibility and I am thankful that it is because I would not be fair to myself. I would give myself much more than what I really need. I would plant thousands of dollars if seed faith offerings were true teaching. It would not make much sense to plant a $500 or $1,000 seed offering if the harvest promised is as we are told. The economics are not adding up. If this is the case then we should pool together and plant covenant seeds.

Wouldn't it be nice if every now and then we would be privileged to hear apologies from our leaders who have taught something wrong and/or erroneous? Seldom will you hear of such a thing. It is almost suggested that ministries have never been subject to erroneous teaching. I really believe that the

Church of God, the body of Christ needs to experience the humble act of pastors repenting and apologizing for teaching wrong principles.

I believe that this new prosperity and faith teaching, which hides behind the wardrobe of God doing a new thing, is error and a tool for prostituting the people of God. Do not let the open and ostentatious show of paying people's bills, buying cars, and paying house notes fool you. Have you ever wondered why it is done in the presence of the church during service? Why not just do it? Do it without ostentation and self-show. Well, if it is done in a private way then politics will not prevail. Many churches give credit to themselves while acclaiming to giving credit to God. There are laws that mandate churches of a certain status to give back to members of that congregation. When gestures of love are presented in front of the congregation, leaders had better make sure that it is not to manipulate others to first, think that they are really doing a God's job and secondly, to influence the congregation to give more. Let us not be fooled when the masses do something mountainous. These things could not be done if the substance was not there. I believe that if the substance (money) dropped off just a little the cause may drop off as well. Showing off in the community and impressing the citizens means but "a hill of beans" if the motive is for self-centered gain. We should never point our fingers at anyone who is what we consider smaller than we are. Instead, let us always remember that **it is not how many we can count but how many God can count on.**

The Bible says in Isaiah 29:24, "They also that erred in spirit shall come to understanding, and they that murmured shall learn doctrine." We, as humans, are all allowed to error. We are not allowed to cover them. Proverbs 28:13 states, "He that covereth his sins shall not prosper: but whoso confesseth and forsaketh them shall have mercy." We cannot afford to cover our sins at the cost of our spiritual character. We often use, "God told me to do something else" in conversation to cover the fact that we have errorred. Misconstrued and erroneous teachings should be addressed as such. The better character admits to error. I wish that God's original ordination for what we do was yet a fresh requirement in our minds. The Lord does not use anything the world or sinners use to signify His gift of prosperity. He uses peace of mind, joy unspeakable, the baptism of power in the Holy Ghost, and revelatory visions and dreams instead. These things cannot be acquired by sinners or through the means of worldliness because they are spiritual substances that place face on our prosperity.

I believe that our prosperity is but a realization of what the Lord predestined for our lives. We, the people of God, have been privileged to possess a spirit that houses a supply, which is adequate to fulfill our needs. We develop our prosperity. The word "shall" is often accompanied by the word prosperity or prospers. This gives us a sense of believing that it has already happened (II Chronicles 20:20, 26:5; Psalm 1:3, 122:6; Isaiah 55:11; Jeremiah 22:30; Judges 18:5; and many more). The message is very clear that God has prospered us since the creation. Our intimate relationship with Him can bring us to this realization. Then, we will not fall into the prostitution schemes and pimping games going on across our pulpits.

Prostitution is one of the oldest professions there is but it is not as old as prosperity. It is only proper that the word prostitution follows the word prosperity in the dictionary. A true and necessary declaration is "What God predestined He purposed with the promise of prosperity." As we grow to trust Him for our development, information, and a prosperous lifestyle, we must also consider His requirements upon our lives. Our motives must be pure and our desires proper. Our virtue must exceed our vanity before it turns into vice and robs us of our victory. Any prosperity attributed to the Lord will have its essence in and from purity and not ill-gotten gain and material abundance. I believe these are some of the reasons that there is a *thin line between prosperity and prostitution.*

It is vital that we understand both the intent and the perspective of this chapter, while trying to stabilize the winds of confusion that may blow from these writings. I wish to use definitions gained from the Webster's Third New International Dictionary for the word *prostitution* and the word *prosperity*. Hopefully, it will be clearly understood that prostitution may birth a type of prosperity but with a startling and disappointing prospectus when prosperity is coveted by means of prostitution. I do borrow from the principles of apologetics as an aid for my writings.

The following definitions are a combination of various forms of the words prosperity and prostitution:

Prosperity	-Attended with or marked by good fortune. Auspicious: doing well. -To succeed in an enterprise or activity. -A state of high general economic activity marked by relatively full employment, an increasing use of resources, and high level of investments.
Prostitution	-To devote to corrupt for an unworthy purpose or end. -A person who deliberately debases himself for money or other considerations.

-A creatively gifted person who deliberately lowers his or her standards for financial gains.

I pray to God for His wisdom in conveying this much needed message of the *thin line between prosperity and prostitution.*

I have found some very interesting points in my studies over the years. None can compete with the points I have discovered in studying prosperity. For instance:

1) Jesus never used the word prosperity.
2) Prosperity is found in only two New Testament scriptures (I Corinthians 16:2 and III John 2).
3) There is not one scripture relative to money as it relates to seed sowing.
4) Conditions are always given for being prosperous and it is not the seed sowing game.

The Bible says in Proverbs 28:3, "A poor man that oppresseth the poor is like a sweeping rain which leaveth no food." Jesus made it clear that His mission on earth most definitely included the condemnation of sin in the flesh (Romans 8:3). Our Lord did not advocate, condone, or cover sin. He exposed it with every intent to heal and save the possessor of it. His goal for mankind, mixed with His purpose for coming to earth as the manifested God, was to clear the pathway between God and His creation, man. This mission did not include the interference from a man-made teaching on prosperity. However, it is here in bold fashion.

Almost every sermon, every revival, and every conference is based around the deceitful suggestion "God wants you to prosper." It is as if people do not know this already. Many people realize that they are not meeting the conditions of God thus they are not necessarily deserving of prosperity. (Thank God for His mercy!) The following is a true yet unattractive question, which is directed toward the character of the church by those who are recruiting members for the wrong reasons. “Do you want to prosper and be allowed to sin at liberty without being challenged to live right? If your answer is “yes” then here is what you must do. Join this ministry and we will show you how.” Thus the games begin. More church members, equal more money received, thus the ministerial concerns become the church’s financial debts being paid off, rather than the development of the church’s character. So, do not be fooled when you hear that a church is debt free. Sin free is what we should be concerned about because this makes us “debt” free.

We should seek God’s face for freedom if this is our mindset toward prosperity. We may have gained a nickel and lost a dime. As a community, it is absolutely flagitious how vulnerable we are to this kind of prostitution. Most people want to be identified as spiritual. If church leaders have the opportunity and the desire, all they really have to do is persuade people by way of their idolatrous spirituality. Then they would have cut out the middleman who would interfere with their scheme to get the people to help them achieve prosperity.

A prostitute, working in that field of service, has lost her self-esteem regardless of how much she lies to herself by stating otherwise. The same is true as it relates to spiritual prostitution. When spiritual esteem is gone we are left vulnerable to prostitution. The message is clear, “If you give me something then I will give you something in return.” As an author I am concerned that God’s Word is being used out of context giving the advantage to prostitution and the game of greed. This leaves the prostitutes void of the opportunity to prosper in the way God has designed for their lives.

These writings are not a collection of stricture with a vindictive foundation. Rather, they are the life rafts for so many people whose hands are still held out waiting on the return on their "investment." We all should feel the truth that lies within the fact that our arms are getting tired and we know that this is not God's ordination for us. **Jesus did not teach prosperity**. It was not important to Him. Based on my relationship with Jesus, prosperity is not first tangible and material, then spiritual. I believe the complete opposite to be true, making our labor insignificant in acquiring the benefits of God, which will develop from our potential. This becomes very clear and evident in my book, *Man, God's Robot.* (Chapters on Potential and Vision)

God finished our lives in predestination with evolvement and development as our tenure. He most certainly did not require us to commit to anything having to do with what is called *seed sowing,* the biggest deception taking place today. (May God forgive me and help me in my ignorance of these matters, if ignorance is the case.) I am going to lose favor among those who say that they are my peers and brothers. I know this. However, I really feel it is my duty, as an apostle, to reveal the error of our ways. The *seed sowing* teaching is a manipulating disparity of the teachings of Jesus.

At times, my writings may appear to be exacerbating. This is not my intended conveyance. Rather, I believe wholeheartedly that we will have to face God. This book represents an opportunity for many to be delivered who may have otherwise been left to drown in their own deceit. This contemporary society is filled with "give to get" schemes. I will take this time to write and share my outlook on what is really taking place.

The birth of prosperity teachings began when Satan offered Jesus all the beauty of the world (St. Matthew 4:8-9; St. Luke 4:5-6). Jesus, God manifested in the flesh, knew that it was neither the proper teaching nor the proper personnel distributing this prosperity. He quickly used the Word to disprove it. His words were, "…Get thee behind me, Satan: for it is written, Thou shalt worship the Lord thy God, and him only shalt thou serve" (St. Luke 4:8). The law is already written. God has not ordained these new interpretations of theology. The multitude and number of people who believe in this entrapment of spiritual distraction is fooling man.

In St. Luke 12:15 we read, "And he said unto them, Take heed, and beware of covetousness: for a man's life consisteth not in the abundance of the things which he possesseth." Notice if you will, the warning in "beware of covetousness," which is defined as marked by inordinate, culpable or envious desire for another's possessions. Some of the synonyms for covetousness are greedy, grasping, and avaricious. The Greek word with its definition is pleonexia (4124), derived from pleon, more and echo (2192), to have. Covetousness is the desire for having more or for what he has not. Contrast philarguria (5365), avarice. Pleonexia is a larger term, which includes philarguria. It is connected with extortioners; with thefts (St. Mark 7:22); with sins of the flesh (Ephesians 5:3; Colossians 3:5). Pleonexia may be said to be the root from which these sins grow, the longing of the creature from which these sins grow and which has forsaken God to fill itself with the lower objects of nature.

Many opinions differ in that the Hebrew definition is more acceptable than the Greek. In my research I find them to be the same in intent. The Hebrew word is beca'-beh'-tsah, from 1214, plunder; by extens. gain (usually unjust): covetousness, (dishonest) gain, lucre, or profit. In Exodus 18:21 we read,

"Moreover thou shalt provide out of all the people able men, such as fear God, men of truth, hating covetousness; and place such over them, to be rulers of thousands, and rulers of hundreds, rulers of fifties, and rulers of tens." This verse tells us to hate covetousness. The devil tried his first message of prosperity against Jesus who knew his character (St. Matthew 4:8-10). There are so many Christians who do not know their character and thus they are always seeking for someone to tell them who they are, as it relates to prosperity. Have we so soon forgotten that we are God's responsibility? Our prosperity is automatically His appetite. Jesus' creditability was important to God. Thus, we have good maintenance on His promises.

In various surveys done throughout the world, prostitutes were asked why they did what they did. The answer at the top of the list was, "the money is good." They mean it "looks" good. (Excuse me for being aggressive by stating what they mean.)

We all know that losing self-respect and self-esteem are still the ultimate of natural losses. Many may gain a negative opinion of me based on my point of view. My prayer is that this will not be the case but rather you will come to appreciate the truth. The word *prostitute* seems appropriate since the church is symbolic of a woman. The world of prostitution travels across the feminine line to all races, creeds, colors, and sex. Prostitution has been adopted as an occupational alternative for many young people, an answer to low paying, low-skilled and boring dead-end jobs, a solution to the high unemployment rate of poor women, and a form of sexual liberation. It is also viewed as a free choice for the career-minded woman.

We should be constantly mindful that *wealth* is sometimes synonymous with *selfishness*. There may be a selfish motive behind each invitation to become wealthy. Most people who teach prosperity will usually do so with their hands open as a gesture for your reward unto them. This may or may not be wrong. We will all need to consider the possibility of ulterior motive and human propensity in judging this matter. It really depends on the motive.

We must consider the words written by the prophet Jeremiah in Jeremiah 6:13 in dealing with the warning of Jesus about covetousness: "For from the least of them even unto the greatest of them every one is given to covetousness; and from the prophet even unto the priest every one dealeth falsely." Jeremiah like Jesus saw the detriment in this monster, covetousness. In Isaiah 57:17, the Prophet Isaiah states that he is wroth (angry) about the iniquity of covetousness. Proverbs 28:16 states that if you hate covetousness you can prolong your days. The Psalmist tells us, in Psalm 119:36, to incline our hearts unto thy testimonies, and not to covetousness. I feel that it is expedient that we read Jeremiah 51:13, "O thou that dwellest upon many waters, abundant in treasures, thine end is come, and the measure of thy covetousness." To epitomize my outlook of today's church, I really would like for you to examine and read Ezekiel 33:31. It reads, "And they come unto thee as the people cometh, and they sit before thee as my people, and they hear thy words, but they will not do them: for with their mouth they show much love, but their heart goeth after their covetousness." The church world seems to be more interested in money and material gain than spirituality.

Holiness is departing from the lips of our pastors, prophets, etc. We seldom hear about holiness except for the misconstrued meaning of the word anointing. May God help us all to escape this vulnerable position of prostitution in order to gain prosperity.

There is little difference between playing the lottery and playing the prosperity game. I once heard a Caucasian pastor teaching on prosperity of the various classes: high, middle and low. (I detest this language.) His statement was when you become "anointed to prosper" (the phrase is erroneous) you will graduate from low class to middle class, then middle class to high class. Everyone applauded. I had two questions: Where do you go from there and what class do you rate the retired older generation that is on a fixed income? I wonder if they qualify for the status of prosperity? Exactly how important is the elderly in your ministry, especially those who have stopped giving because they have no more to give? Can they still sit on the front row or are all of the seats filled with diplomats, professional athletes, movie stars, and entrepreneurs? The elderly do not "sin" much, yet they cannot seem to prosper. Maybe we should lay our anointed hands on them that they can hear our teachings about how to give more. Maybe they should sow a seed offering to receive good health. Forgive me for my sarcasm but I am fed up with the lies and manipulating schemes about seed sowing and prosperity. The truth is that many pastors do not care about those who are not resourceful or capable of giving.

Pastors and leaders are therefore admonished to deal with truth through the eyes of holiness although it may incriminate them. Many church leaders have drifted. Money has become their god. They only fellowship with greed (brother) and covetousness (sister) and they call it "eagles not wanting to live with the chickens." May I remind you that eagles do not supply life to humanity as chickens do. It is not so bad being a chicken if it means staying with God. We must remember that this is not the teaching of Jesus but the teaching of economic strategy and prosperity programs. Jesus fellowshipped with the chickens.

Here is a challenging question, "By whose definition are the eagles better than the chickens anyway?" You will not become a chicken by hanging with chickens any more than Jesus became a winebibber by fellowshipping with winebibbers. The idea of flying high like an eagle is attractive but the impact from the fall could be devastating. Also, becoming extinct is a grave and frightening possibility.

Prostitutes get caught up in prostitution for the same reason countries get caught in war and economics, money. We should all examine the effects of this profession on the one who practices the trade. While prostitution is a service industry that exists, prosperity teaching, outside the will of God, exists for the sole purpose of "giving to get." A professional call girl must turn off her feelings and become an object for others to relieve their sexual insatiability. A preacher turned actor must turn off his feelings and become an object, used by the devil, to promise relief to those in covetous practices with gain and ungodliness on their minds. A prostitute becomes disillusioned about love and romance because she realizes that her value is purely physical and when that wears out, she is valueless. A Christian being deceived by prosperity teachings may feel a sense of significance at first (based on material and tangibles), but eventually his value will drop when he realizes that everything is going down but the Word of God (Isaiah 40:7).

Prostitution is emotionally difficult and physically dangerous. Erroneous prosperity teachings without a pure biblical foundation is spiritually damaging and could become irreparable. While prostitution carries the threat of AIDS with it, the church world has the bigger concern of missing God.

Again, I must refer to the teachings of Jesus. In St. Luke 12:15b we read, "...for a man's life consisteth not in the abundance of the things which he possesseth." The word abundance deserves consideration. In St. John 10:10, Jesus states that He came that we might have life, and have it more abundantly. This has been used to support more gain, more money and more of the material desires of our hearts. That is not what God meant (if I may). The subject discussed was "life" not material abundance. Life! That is why it is not a contradiction when we hear Him state that a man's life consisteth not in the "abundance of things" which he possesseth.

During the temptation in the wilderness, Jesus was offered what He already had (St. Matthew 4:1-11). The devil is yet trying to offer us what is already ours. **We will start living when we realize that prosperity is developed from our potential. It is not reaped from a harvest.** Except for justifiable explanations, there are no relative scriptures that outline prosperity as a need for success.

Why did leaders have to go and mess up the Word with revisions? First, they denounced the authenticity of the King James Edition as the original text. Then, they trusted any and everybody to write new kinds of bibles because of a need to justify erroneous teachings. Now we cannot seem to stop this snowball of deceit. There is too much pride involved and not enough humility to substantiate the need for repentance.

I believe that the biggest issue for a preacher is not knowing where the money will come from if he stops prostituting the people of God. Many pastors plunged into debt stating that God led them to do this or that, and now they feel that prostitution methods are needed for survival.

I am just a voice crying in the wilderness. I hope God will allow someone to hear my cries. Let us get back to holiness, praying at the altar, and having revivals without money as the motive. Let the stewards and deacons take up the offering instead of the preacher. Let the preacher prepare to preach. Why do we really ask the pastor to minister the offering anyway?

PROSTITUTION AND LIFTING THE OFFERING

The procedures used in lifting the offering may have a slight hint of prostitution. Let us examine this situation. Why is it necessary for the one preaching to take up the offering? Is the motive raising a certain amount of money, and are we using the manipulation strategy of personality persuasion? Was the invitation to preach given and accepted based on a monetary vision? The answer to these three questions demand a humble spirit and a desire to get better at who we are as the agents of the Lord.

I believe that the true motive to the first question may be a strategy to raise money. We have studied the mentality of people so much that we understand the law of getting them to give toward our programs. The tools used for subtle prostitution are, emotion and need. Leaders have discovered that "emotional" people will most likely give more freely. Thus, it becomes the job of the person receiving the honorarium to evoke the emotions of the people. This is an assumed knowledge between the speaker and the invitor.

While this may be defined as economical strategy, it still needs our observation and scrutiny to make sure it is not a preconceived act of prostitution of God's people. People are very vulnerable when they are emotional. This is not a license to take advantage of them. A promise of a future harvest during an emotional time only adds to their willingness to give. This exchange can be defined as an act of prostitution. (Not all cases are applicable.) I really believe that a simple explanation of our need is sufficient to encourage giving if profit and extreme gain are not our goal.

I do not intend to send the message of a ruthless and radical attack. However, I believe that all a man needs to survive is an opportunity. He bases his choice to survive on his will to change the state of his situation. If this is the case, then everyone reading this book will see it as an opportunistic gift from the Lord. While this is not true in every case, it is enough for me to sense the need for writing and explaining our vulnerable states to this fast growing spirit of prostitut-ion. The following questions and answers are some clues why I am concerned about this matter:

1. What is the size of your congregation?
   My reply, "Why does that matter?"
2. What is your monetary vision?
   My reply, "Excuse me, don't you want to know my spiritual vision?"
3. Will I be staying in a four-star or five-star hotel?
   My reply, "And if not, would you still come?"
4. Will a limousine be picking me up?
   My reply, "It may be a truck if it's okay with you?"
5. I'll need to fly first class.
   My reply, "Even if you fly coach, you will still be first class."

I truly believe that there are better and more spiritual ways to deal with these scenarios. The size of the congregation should not be important. It is not wise to extend your services just to satisfy another ministry's desire to prostitute you because of your ability to draw people to their setting. For instance, you are in New York and a church in Atlanta invites you to come but it cannot afford to supply the needs for your travel. Then it would not be expedient to go unless you feel lead to go instead of the church asking you to come.

I like the idea of asking churches that ask me to come and preach, but are financially incapable of bearing the expense, to come and fellowship at my church with me on a day that is convenient for them, since it is my preaching that they say they really want. Too often this is not the case. They too want to prostitute me. One may travel with a hundred people or a thousand, and this number of people might mean a good offering especially if it is noised abroad that he is a free giver and teach the same. It is a shame, the things that have happened to our Christian community. This is why I write that there is a *thin line between prostitution and prosperity.* I won't fail to mention that my message would be very much appreciated if I told people that they are going to prosper, drive new cars, get new homes, get new jobs, husbands will return, ministries will be restored, etc. Where is God's will for our lives in all of this? Isn't it true that all we really want to do is please God?

I wish that we had programs that do not include money exchanges. At the church where I pastor, the pastor's, the evangelist's, or the speaker's honorarium is prepared before the service ever starts, thus freeing the church from any pressure to raise a certain amount of money. I have never held a service of any kind for the sole purpose of raising money. I think that service and fellowship ought to be free from games and money schemes.

I remember an occasion where I invited a group of pastors for a week of fellowship. I made it very clear what we could afford to give as an honorarium. We all agreed to the amount. (I think it was somewhere between $300 and $500.) I knew that some of these speakers were prosperity oriented and I did not want a conflict with my disagreement of these teachings. It was fixed and settled. They agreed to come and I agreed to them coming. One particular night things were going well until offering time. The pastor asked me if he could take up the offering for the service. I told him, "No, that's okay. We already have it taken care of." He looked disgruntled and said, "Okay, if that's what you want." It seemed to disturb him that he could not freely pimp the people through the offering. I could sense a little friction and a little tension, so I prayed his disturbance would not grow. I knew that he had to preach and I did not want to disturb that fact. He preached and did a good job. Every now and then he would refer to what God was going to do for our ministry, which to us was an affirmation and not a confirmation. Preachers often think that that is a part of their job. Most of the messages sound the same: God is going to bless you; this ministry is going to grow, get ready to build. If there is no musician, it is always proper to say, "God is going to send an anointed musician," you know, the kind of stuff that can bring about an emotional joy. While I understand intent, I am afraid that we may overlook satanic strategy.

The preaching of the gospel is not only about making one happy but also about setting one free. Slowly but surely, we are losing sight of our divine calling, which is the spreading of the Gospel, the condemning of sin in the flesh, the restoration of hope in Christ and the reconciliation of our spiritual and intimate relationships with God. Sadly, I must say that for the love of money Christians are becoming evil (I Timothy 6:10). If our motive is to raise money then we have failed at our calling. If we are under so much debt that we know of no other way out then we should re-check the foundation of our stewardship. It is okay to stop, change, and save the congregation. Do not become a pimp under the auspices of a ministry, soliciting the service of a renowned speaker as a prostitute for the fulfillment of an economical desire, while taking the souls of God's people as clienteles.

I will give credit to some of our renowned pastors. Many will preach to any size congregation as long as the money is right. There are many invitations that I have turned down because some ministries will use the visiting pastor for the wrong motive, prostitution. If I discern an impure motive then I will require knowing the occasion for the invitation. If it is for the purpose of fundraising then I will not allow myself to become a tool for fundraising. There are other means that we could use without prostituting God's people for our financial prosperity. It really bothers me to think that I might be prostituted. Every pastor should consider his dignity rather than gain.

Many of us know that we are being prostituted but our very own prosperity is a greater interest and we are not willing to change that. Consider this scenario:

A preacher received $10,000 for preaching a one-night revival (and believe me this is a very small amount compared to some of the honorariums given at a certain church). He was asked to come again the following year, but the church membership had decreased. The church was willing to cover all expenses, however the honorarium would only be $1,000. The church felt that there was a chance that the preacher would not come. As it turned out his schedule was too crowded and the response letter included, "I am sorry but I really would like to come. Call me at a later time."

The problem lies in the foundation of the precedence. When we sow prostitution we reap the disease of unscrupulous character. Believe me I do understand that "birds of a feather flock together." I would like to rebut by saying, "For wheresoever the carcass is, there will the eagles be gathered together" (St. Matthew 24:28).

Another issue I wish to discuss is the monetary vision behind the invitation. We often hear a reply of a 60/40 offering split, "Get me $10,000 and the rest is yours," or "You can take up your own offering" to placate the image of greed. Traveling evangelists often drool at the idea of taking up their own offerings. The image is very clear, in my mind, of a wolf while licking his lips at the idea of having all those vulnerable sheep at his disposal, just waiting on a word from the Lord so they can pay for it. Let us not forget that even Palm Readers and Psychics "hit" every now and then. You cannot miss when speaking generalities. For instance, saying that somebody in the service has a headache, a lower backache, a heart murmur, swelling in their legs, or migraines are general assumptions and not a word of prophecy or a word from the Lord.

The prostitute reads your mind by watching your face. Be very careful because if you respond then you are going to be called out. The prostitute wears the kind of clothes that will entice you to believe him. The dress apparel is not flamboyant or ostentatious. He wears one ring to demonstrate modesty and dresses in sacred-looking attire to "go get them." People love to think that they can actually discern a preacher's character while overlooking the fact that they do not have an intimate relationship with the Lord, outside of hypocrisy in fooling others to think so.

I make it a habit to ask the congregation to ask the Lord if I am a man of God or not before I begin ministering. One lady told me she would have to wait until later on in the service. (I thought to myself, "If you are that much in order with God, why not discern it now?") What she really wanted was to see if my preaching was agreeable with her. Then, I would be a man of God. Needless to say it was not. I perceived her evil intent and preached the unadulterated Word of God. It is not given to man to judge God's vessels. When we do, we are taking on the role of a god.

My interest is the spiritual vision of the church and not the money. Church has almost become a lottery-type operation. Playing the numbers game has been changed to playing the personality game. Spiritual leaders were not like this in the beginning. They have left their first love (Revelation 2:4). Filthy lucre and ill-gotten gain is their greed, covetousness is their wardrobe, and renownedness is the transportation. Revivals should not be about raising money.

Nothing bothers me more and insults me greater than a church trying to give me a lesser honorarium than they gave or proposed to give to another pastor or evangelist, especially when I am filling in for the one who could not come. This proves that the church's concern is money and not spirituality.

Once I traveled out of the country to preach at this megachurch. While having dinner I was asked about my expenses. I responded, "Just make them even with the last person's." I knew that a very renowned speaker had just ministered there. After convincing the people of the fact that God was going to bless them, the renowned speaker left. Now, here I was. I preached revival into their souls. This I state in accordance with their testimonies. My honorarium was very small compared to the renowned speaker's, but it was adequate enough for me to survive. I was happy and the church was blessed with the "true" kind of blessing. A revelation from the Word of God was shared and revival came to the hearts of the people. I am sure that you can see my point.

This thing has gotten out of control and I have been given the assignment to write about it. One critic told me that he could hear my anger when he read my writings. This is very far from being true if he means that I am angry towards people. However, I am angry towards the devil's work in the body of Christ.

Do you really think that I like the idea of being called a radical, an anti-us, or a prosperity parasite? Certainly not! I am guilty of having a greater love for pleasing God than a greed for friendship. I must admit that I sometimes long to hear encouragement from my peers. My prayer is, "Lord, give me friends that will scripturally disprove my teachings if I am in error. I will then apologize to all men for being in error. I only ask the same of the rest of my peers, "Fix what you mess up and please the Lord in doing so." We do not have a chance at recovering what we have lost if we continue to add insult to injury.

My passion to write is unexplainable and very challenging. I have never done well with hypocrisy, although I have had my days as well. It is just not worth it trying to please people when you are displeasing the Lord. This book suggests that there is a conquest between holiness and a whole lot of mess, and what used to be and what is now. I am convinced that there is a *thin line between prosperity and prostitution.*

One of the questions that I proposed earlier was relative to the lodging expense for evangelists and pastors when they go to a city for the purpose of preaching the gospel. Why is it necessary to stay in a four or five-star hotel? (I am not sure of the reason for wanting to do so.) I will say that this elaborate and exquisite living is perceived as a vital part of prosperity. With this in mind, I will add another issue to our discussion. It deals with a limousine as transportation from the airport. These requests are absolutely ridiculous and should be the choice of the host (within reason) and not the demand of the guest.

Have we forgotten that it is all about Jesus and God being glorified and not self-glorification? I have gained recognition from the *God Can God Will Ministries* television ministry and various revivals. As long as God knows who I am then nothing else matters. I think that we should be concerned with our accommodations but it does not necessarily have to be a four or five-star hotel. The disease here is the precedence that is set; if you do for me then I am compelled to do for you.

Based on the opinions that I share in this book and the incriminating effect that they may have in some ministers' lives many will encourage their members to stay away from my writings and me because, "He is crazy, ignorant, and does not know what he's talking about." In actuality, this book is the "rain on the parade" of erroneous prosperity teachings, which are based on prostituting the people of God for self-gain playing the "give to get" game. We have been promised a "jubilee" and we should know by now that it will never happen, outside of our justifiable explanation. We are told that we are anointed, while overlooking our common-law lifestyles and practices. I understand why one may attack my writings but this has not convinced me to stop. We owe it to the people to tell them the truth.

Another question posed earlier referred to first class or coach flights. The difference between first class and coach is so small in variation that this really should not matter, except of course, those who ride in first class portray a certain image to the onlooker. They are perceived as very important. God's agents are always important regardless of the section of the airplane they fly in. When I think of the goodness of Jesus and all He has done for me, it compels me to become dedicated, devoted, and devout. My interest is not money and gain but rather souls and their development, growth, and spiritual stability. I challenge all other agents of God to meet me on this level.

Order is the essence of prosperity. Greed is its vice. We are prone to being insatiable thus vulnerable to deception. It is easy to overlook the fact that we must all stand before God and we must give an account for the things that we have done. He has already promised to supply our need. That one need is His Spirit, which controls all else. Our character needs more class than charisma and our personality needs more power than performance. I write this book because I believe that the characteristics of the kingdom emanate from the character of the king. If we coerce people to believe in fake and façade then their destiny will be frivolity and fortuitousness, which will force them to live beneath the spiritual privilege that God has promised. We should not approach these writings myopically.

In God's Word, He makes it very clear that it is His responsibility that we prosper (Genesis 24:40; 39:3; 39:23; Deuteronomy 29:9). In I Kings 2:3, we are given conditions for prosperity, which have absolutely nothing to do with seed sowing. In Numbers 14:41 Moses shows us that transgression will curse prosperity. Prosperity is very attractive but it should not be an item for prostitution. There is a thin line between the two, prosperity and prostitution, when considering the nuances. Normally, these minute variations would not matter but in this case they are very important because a little leaven can leaven the whole lump.

In Psalm 1, we are given very strict conditions for prosperity. We are told not to walk in the counsel of the ungodly, nor stand in the way of sinners, nor sit in the seat of the scornful.

If these conditions are met we are promised to be like a tree planted by the rivers of water. We will constantly bring forth fruit in due season. Our leaves will not wither and whatever we do will prosper. In Psalm 73:3, the psalmist mentions the prosperity of the wicked. In the twelfth verse of the same division, the wicked are referred to as ungodly, prosperous in the world, and have increase in riches. It is therefore blatant prostitution when a wicked scheme is used to gain and acquire money, using the people of God to do so while promising them that if they give they will get. All of our getting will be based on God's will for our lives. He wants us to prosper and be in health (III John 2). However, we must remember that this is in proportion to prosperity in the spiritual things of God.

For the sake of our own security, we are told not to fret because of many who are prospering in what they are doing, although they may be doing wrong, for they will soon be cut down like the grass and wither as the green herb (Psalm 37:1-2). The book of Job has a very encouraging scripture, "If they obey and serve him, they shall spend their days in prosperity, and their years in pleasures"(Job 36:11). I wish to encourage all men to live the example given in Psalm 30:6, which reads, "And in my prosperity I said, I shall never be moved." Most men cannot do this. Their greed gains momentum from their human propensity and they will move away from God as a first love taking on the desire for money. Proverbs 1:32 warns that the prosperity of fools shall destroy them. Before I close this section, I wish to echo again that Jesus said a man's life does not consist in the abundance of the things which he possess (St. Luke 12:15).

GIVING VERSUS GAME

We should all beware of "games." This word is somewhat slang. It means a style of doing something, usually with something else in mind. I believe that there is a very thin line between giving and gaming. Whenever numbers are used in giving it is gaming. For instance money lines, prayer lines that cost, selling prophecies, selling anointed oil, and many more little tricks are tried in the church.

One day during the offering ministry, a female preacher said, "Men always want to be in charge. Now is the time for them to be the head. I want all *real* men to give twenty dollars in the offering." That is pure, blatant game. A young man is gaming when he perpetrates an image of talking on a cellular phone when his service is disconnected. A fake business card is gaming. A young person literally crying tears to get an advantage in conversation is gaming. Giving a pager number instead of a phone number because of one's true marital status is gaming. Showing a wad of money with a major bill exposed, whent there are only one-dollar bills underneath is called gaming. Wearing fake jewelry is gaming. Repeating a sermon as if it is yours is called gaming. Going to bed late on purpose so you will not have to be intimate with your companion is called gaming. The 1-900-sex lines are all games. Wrestling is gaming. There are so many more.

The biggest of all games take place in the Christian community under the name of "giving" in the church. A pastor peeps out of his study and notices that there are only about one hundred people in service. The budget is $5,000 according to his financial advisors who are also present with him in his study. To reach this goal, each person will be asked to give fifty dollars. The crowd increases to two hundred a few minutes later therefore knocking the individual amount down to twenty-five dollars. Finally, there are about five hundred people present, which makes everyone unknowingly responsible for ten dollars. However, profit must be considered, so the leader asks, "Oh did we consider our profit?" Someone out of the group states that the profit is already considered in the budget. The crowd is real "juicy" and ready to give. It is obvious, because they are hungry for a special word from the Lord. (Every Word from God should be special.) Maybe the pastor will cheat just a little and ask everyone to give twenty dollars for a little extra profit. They will never know the difference.

People who game themselves are always looking for "something for nothing" so they are prime candidates for being gamed. Now, the game is to ask at least ten people to give five hundred dollars, twenty people to give two hundred and fifty dollars, fifty people to give one hundred dollars, one hundred people to give fifty dollars, two hundred and fifty people to give twenty dollars and the rest whatever they can. Too much time is spent playing this game. If we add all of the figures, we should get about thirty thousand dollars for a five thousand dollar budget. This game is never perfect but its goal is to reach at least half of the thirty thousand dollars. (Note that the preacher's honorarium comes from this amount.) Sometimes they will still take up a preacher's offering. Gaming is purely unspiritual, unbiblical and unethical, but it is being used in many churches. Every service should be based on our hunger for God and not the budget.

God will reward our services with the monies we need if we would stop gaming the people. The evangelist is asked to take up the offering because his deal is a 50/50 split. For those of you who do not know, this means the evangelist gets fifty percent of the monies collected and the other fifty-percent goes to the church. In many cases these services are based on fundraising, which makes them "game."

How have leaders become so unscrupulous with the ministry? The answer could very well be from following the crowd. Young pastors are ruined when they sit in the midst of unspiritual pastors who have the status of being anointed. If a person does not have the strength within himself to say, "no" to these practices then he will succumb to them. Asking for what is needed and telling what has been received should determine the giving. The other kind of behavior is all a numbers game. In this case the Spirit is absent from our motives and it is not a part of our efforts to please the Lord.

Lifting the offering is important in service. It should not become a game we play. "For the love of money is the root of all evil…"(I Timothy 6:10). This kind of "game play" will not stop until the Holy Ghost is put in charge again. Many fellowships are really prostitution swaps of money to the preacher's advantage. For instance, when I travel to a church to preach a sermon and I am asked to take up an offering, I must realize that those more willing to give will be the members of my church who accompany me. Their giving will go to me in the form of an honorarium with the rest left there at the church. In many cases, the pastor who asks his people to travel with him will know in advance that they are being prostituted and will still allow it because the agreement has reciprocity. In other words, the favor of pimping my people will be returned to me in the form of pimping your people. It behooves us to remember that these are all God's people. Again, let me say that fellowship should not be for the purpose of raising money.

I do not fair well in the ministerial arena among my peers because I reject the idea of promoting the offering. I do on certain occasions minister the offering just because I am the speaker. This suggests that I am the prostitute and since I am the one "table dancing" for the moment, then I am the one to ask the client to give. I must say that I demand purity and integrity in doing so. I play no games, absolutely no games! I thank God that I'm this way. I guess I am like Paul about baptism; it is not my calling. My conversion is not my calling. My charisma and influence is not my calling. Here is my point. Who told the church community that it is alright to game people under the auspice of fellowship? My character does not include the game play of money through fellowship.

If I ask a man to preach for me based on his ability to draw a crowd, am I not prostituting him and pimping the people? The people will come because the "preacher" will be there. They will give because he asks them to. They give, he gets his percentage, the people get an emotional high and then he leaves until the next engagement. It is all game.

If a man chooses to come to your facility to preach a message in the name of Jesus and in the power of the Holy Ghost then he should be compensated for his service and rewarded for his works. This should be the responsibility of the host ministry. If the congregation is participating in the expense of this relationship, they should be knowledgeable of the budget. They should not be coerced to give toward the occasion as a category in numbers but as cheerful givers. The Lord will honor this effort and release His already predestined will for the occasion. The evangelist sticks to his calling, the pastor maintains good character, the church is left pristine, the people are spiritually fed, and most of all, the Lord is glorified. There is no game in this kind of service. It is our fault as pastors for allowing ourselves to be gamed thus gaming others.

Leaders should stop this "speaking a word" game that is going on in the church, which is mostly guesswork and the rest is obvious. The Lord does not speak through everyone that preaches. He satisfies His will many times with just the delivery of His Word. I believe in "ask and it shall be given." If the Lord leads us to ask then we are going to get what we ask for. The trouble is that much of our asking is based on greed. I have never considered money in our crusades or revivals. I am not privy to the financial gain or loss from a crusade because money is not an interest or my calling. Financial matters are the responsibility of the stewards. This is not my goal.

I know that it is right to reward an evangelist for his work. However, we are looking for rewards according to our renownedness. This in my opinion is a travesty, thus it is my passion to write and share these truths. The popularity of this book is not as important as its conveyance of necessary truths.

The truth is, renownedness equals many people, which equals much money, which means people are given to think that this is the way it works. Always remember that whenever an honorarium gets into the thousands of dollars, it is the thousands that determine the acceptance of the invitation. This is a really sad state for the church. It is all game. Traveling evangelists are demanding four and five star hotels, limos, valet service and catering, in many cases. Oh, let us not forget that they must have a suite. Why is all of that necessary? Mind you, it is not wrong if the intent is pure but is it necessary? Most of these unnecessary amenities are based on game. Jesus, the greatest of all givers, did not demand elaborate and extravagant things. Although the world is His and the fullness thereof, He never flaunted it. There was no game in His ministry. He only cared about people's souls.

In these last days, the opposite is true. Souls do not seem to matter as much as economics. I may stand alone with the belief that the church should never have allowed herself to be classified as a business. I believe that this has diluted our pristine spirituality. We must get rid of the game and work towards giving God the glory. We cannot afford to lose our sense of time and place. When we stop our individual conscious thinking, and our minds become oblivious to our surroundings, this can be called a borderline hypnotic state of mind.

Our participation in these games shows our allowance of them even though we know that they are wrong. Why is this allowed to take place? Why allow these games to go on? This altered state of mind, while appearing to be natural, can be induced by clever manipulation. Testimonies about prosperity are distractions that our "eyes" focus on in order to induce a vulnerable state to the game that is being played. In my opinion, one of the purposes of evangelical renownedness is to reduce any resistance to the game of giving by stopping all contrary thoughts and analogies. If we look close enough, we can see the game in many forms. My concern is this, gaming may not be consciously perceived. Every little trick used to induce giving can be an adopted principle. This adoption can carry into every facet of our lives leaving us vulnerable to anything and anyone.

Giving should not come with game. I Corinthians 16:1-2 reads, "Now concerning the collection for the saints, as I have given order to the churches of Galatia, even so do ye. Upon the first day of the week let every one of you lay by him in store, as God hath prospered him, that there be no gatherings when I come." Let us consider the words "as God hath prospered him." This phrase gives a clear message that we are not to practice giving to get. We should give from the realization that we are already prosperous. In return, we will have access to more and more of this prosperity. This will compliment our cheerfulness in giving. Our giving should be a matter of daily prayer, according to the leading of God, to the glory of Christ, and keeping a constant consciousness that the earth is the Lord's and the fullness thereof (Psalm 24:1). Giving should be done in support of the ministry to take care of the Lord's work, which blesses Christians and offers them spiritual help. We find this principle in Galatians 6:6, "Let him that is taught in the word communicate unto him that teacheth in all good things."

The word *communicate* is translated as sharing and refers to Christian giving. One should always give financial, material and tangible help to the preacher or teacher who helps him spiritually. This principle is clearly taught in I Corinthians 9:9-14, "For it is written in the law of Moses, Thou shalt not muzzle the mouth of the ox that treadeth out the corn. Doth God take care for oxen? Or saith he it altogether for our sakes? For our sakes, no doubt, this is written: that he that ploweth should plow in hope; and that he that thresheth in hope should be partaker of his hope. If we have sown unto you spiritual things, is it a great thing if we shall reap your carnal things? If others be partakers of this power over you, are not we rather? Nevertheless we have not used this power; but suffer all things, lest we should hinder the gospel of Christ. Do ye not know that they which minister about holy things live of the things of the temple? and they which wait at the altar are partakers with the altar? Even so hath the Lord ordained that they which preach the gospel should live of the gospel."

The Bible clearly teaches that those who are blessed by the preaching and teaching of the gospel are to support it. We all have an obligation to support the pastor and the church where we are spiritually fed and blessed, as well as any television and radio gospel broadcasts that feed us spiritually. These broadcasts can either be from our own ministries of others. Our minds must be clear of all games if we are to maintain a pure line of thought for our giving. We must be very careful what we read and watch on television because any repetitious concept can lead to an altered state of vulnerability.

A hypnotist uses a patterned speech by varying the pace and inflexion in his voice to induce a particular state of mind in his subject. This also occurs when, erroneous ecclesiastical voices, filled with statements of what the Lord said and what the word God has for you, subtly massage their congregants with patterned speech. Once the congregation has been soothed into a state of mind to listen they are most susceptible to mental programming. If God says that He will give me a house, which makes me happy, then when He asks me to give one hundred dollars I should not become mad and resistant. The emotion from the promise of a house has trapped me into giving one hundred dollars.

An individual becomes trapped by this game of giving if he trusts the source of the information and if he is exposed to repetition of that same information. Thus, we have the answer to our "cliquish" fellowship.

I was told the book I authored entitled, *Man, God's Robot* was not welcomed in a particular bookstore. I thought that the book would be given a fair placement in a supposedly black-owned bookstore in our community. However, the content of the book admonishes money schemes and seed sowing games, so I was told that this concept was not what they believe. When I looked at the list of renowned authors whose books were allowed in the bookstore, the thought of how many people are being deceived to think that they can sow a seed in the form of a dollar and reap a harvest scared me. This is blatant game and error. It is possible that prosperity, as it is defined by our secular society, will flourish in the midst of Biblical contradiction. It is not fair to the universal reader if we ostracize reading material that contradicts the error within the seed sowing teaching.

People need a chance to make a proper and knowledgeable choice. When we place too much trust in the source of the information, it will automatically induce acceptance and lend us the responsibility of believing that the information is true even though it may not have been understood. Further, we will be given to think that it cannot be wrong under any circumstance. All men are wrong sometimes. For sure, all have sinned and fallen short of the glory of God (Romans 3:23).

Repetition of error imbeds that error into the subconscious so that acceptance of its "truth" becomes a conditioned response regardless of its inaccuracy. Now, almost anytime you are told to participate in any type of giving, you will do it under the influence of this error. Unfortunately, many who have awakened to the fact that they have been influenced by the game of giving, vow never to give again. Therefore, in the midst of honest effort they will be paranoid about giving to anyone else. I am writing this book to try and save someone, anyone from this game of giving. There is *a thin line between giving and game.*

CON-ARTISTRY OR CONSECRATION

I have spent time with the Lord God in very intimate ways therefore I feel somewhat adept in the nature of consecration. I have received many revelations from hours in consecration, some that can be uttered and others that cannot. I take pride in knowing that I have been "set apart." It makes me feel humble and I pay homage to the Lord God for thinking enough of me to choose me as one of His true worshippers (St. John 4:23).

I think that it may be safe for me to say and write that I have spent time with Him whom I worship. I also recognize that the Lord God is requiring worship by means of consecration. The thief who has come to steal, to kill, and to destroy (St. John 10:10) has done so by persuading men to think that they are worshipping the Lord God without a life of consecration. Again, I want to emphasize that those of us who are the worshippers of God are the choices of God. God has chosen certain people who will consecrate themselves to be His true worshippers and willingly worship Him in spirit as well as in truth. This truth does not demand perfection and sinlessness but it does demand purity in our confessions. I believe that if we only understood that God understands who we are, we would then have a straight line to God, making it easy to understand how passionate and compassionate He is about those He has chosen to worship Him.

Jesus makes it very clear in St. John 4:23 that God is seeking "such" to worship Him. I liken this to the mornings when I ride by certain street corners and there are groups of men waiting to be sought by an employer who needs help for the day. They stand there and eventually someone will come by and ask them if they want to make a day's wage. The answer is, "Yes." They will then get in the person's truck, go to work and make a day's wage.

The Lord God is constantly walking in the garden of man's life, seeking for the opportunity to ask, "... who then is willing to consecrate his service this day unto the Lord?" (I Chronicles 29:5) We are encompassed with so much materialistic and tangible substance that it takes spiritual concentration to maintain divine consecration. It is easy to lose sight of the essence of God; all men have at some time or another. His true nature is spiritual and is not to be physically touched or perceived. It is spiritual and should be understood as such.

God is a Spirit and those who aspire to be the worshippers spoken of in St. John 4:23, as being sought by Him, must align themselves with the truth of His word. In speaking of the *thin line between con-artistry and consecration*, it becomes a mandate that when we confess we do so in honesty as well as earnestness. This act lets the Lord God know that it is our desire to deny the human inflicted part of us that is so contrary to His will, so that we may gain access to His Spirit to become worshippers and to be classified as consecrated.

Consecration is vital for continuity, constancy, and consistency. People often operate from their idea of God but in reality it is not God's plan for them. There are many people who start and then stop. Then, there are others who are consistent only at being inconsistent. Imagine God choosing this kind of person as a true worshipper, depending on him to always be set apart for Himself, only to discover that this person has not willed himself to be available to God, unless of course God operates on that individual's time. I do not think that He could keep up His image as God if He trusted us with the rules and laws that we are governed by as it relates to consecration.

Another true entity of consecration is dedication, which is exclusively devoted to the service or worship of God in hopes of being used in His sacred needs such as using our hands to touch the head of the one He wants to heal. Dedication is not only to devote exclusively but also to recognize that we have been set apart, sanctified unto holiness, and this fact should be the basis for our consistency and constancy in Him. To be dedicated is to commit to something as a constant goal or way of life, to inscribe, to surrender to public use. With these explanations of the word dedication in mind, we justify our asking our consecrated lives to be set apart. Availability for public use may cause us to preach in the streets, or go to the hospitals and lay hands on the sick, go to convalescent homes, to be abused after taking a stand, or to be talked about and ridiculed for preaching the word of God.

Sometimes, dedication is distinguished from consecration as in the dedication of Solomon's temple. That was a totally different kind of dedication. The dedication referred to in this book is an entity of consecration. I am trying to be as intricate as I can because of the sacredness and the seriousness of the subject of consecration. We will talk about con-artistry in a moment. Hopefully, the easiness in becoming a con-artist, being hypocritical in consecration, and inevitably losing out with the Lord because of the hypocrisy in one's worship will be explained.

Dedication is self-sacrificing devotion. Dedication includes the yielding of our zeal and our faithfulness as well as our enthusiasm. When we are consecrated to the Lord, we are controlled by Him, governed by His Spirit, and are His robots. When we experience enthusiasm and zeal as the choices of God, we shine as the light of the world giving God the glory (St. Matthew 5:14). Notice that all of these requirements upon our lives have needed the assistance of our human flesh or the agreement of our natural inclinations. It seems as if the Lord has chosen us to be true worshippers so He has given us this ability to deny ourselves and follow Him, to consecrate ourselves, and to always be there for Him when He needs us. This is the ultimate of compliment. I think that if we would spend more time dedicating ourselves to the Lord and consecrating our spirits, we would then realize just how prosperous we are in that position alone. What a major status! Everyone who sees us and everyone who knows us, will know us as the consecrations of the Lord or, let me say, as the persons set aside for the Lord's use.

The difference between devotion and dedication is not very much unless of course we want to add the word devout. You see, devotion usually includes giving up something (time, money, thought, effort, etc.) for the cause or for the benefit of, for the advancement of something regarded as deserving support. This is different from dedication to a certain extent. Dedication may not require giving up one's possessions but devotion includes the actual act of giving them up and desiring to dedicate everything one has to the secondary status of life, giving the Lord the primary love out of one's heart.

Sometimes we are asked to center our attention on God's activities alone. He specifies certain places to go and certain things to do in order to develop our consecration. When we are consecrated we are delivered up or we are given over with deepest solemnity, dedication, and devotion. I think God recognizes us when we have reached this consecrated state. I think that we miss this point. We are not able to distinguish, especially from one another and often from ourselves, when we have reached the consecrated state. Sometimes we have dedicated certain things to the Lord and we think this automatically means consecrated. This is not necessarily true.

Every consecration is an ordination or an elevation to a higher office or a higher level in God. So, if a person is consecrated then he or she should have no problem understanding why those who have not dedicated or devoted themselves are not doing the things that they should be doing. It is on a higher level that we are able to look down for the purpose of picking up and helping others, and to see just how far the Lord has allowed us to go on the basis of our commitment and consecration to Him. It is on the next level that we learn our job descriptions as being those who praise and worship the Lord. Our whole creation, our whole purpose is to please and praise the Lord. Oh how I pray that my life can adopt these principles, pleasing and praising the Lord. It is not just poetry. It is not just verbiage. It is my heart's desire for the Lord to help me to please Him, and teach me how to praise Him.

In Exodus 28:41, there are three things, three elements given that seem to be the qualifications for ministry. They are anoint, consecrate, and sanctify. While all three of these are categorically the same, they all have their very special function.

The anointing of the Lord is a shield by which God has vowed to protect us. The sanctification of the Lord is a signification to those that the Lord has promised to always be with. A consecration is a passport to those that God has personally chosen to be His worshippers. It is at this time that our behavior and our gestures become ministry. So often I see people do what they call praise the Lord and I say to myself, "I wonder if they know what praising the Lord is all about? Do they understand that everything that has breath can give adoring and admiring compliments to the Lord but that does not distinguish them from others?" A drunkard has "breath" therefore he can raise his hands above his head and give the Lord compliments and the Lord would honor the fact that that drunkard recognizes his undeserving yet merciful life span. We are no more special than the drunkard or his likeness just because we can raise our hands and express compliments unto the Lord.

The definition that we give ourselves, which is filled with logic, reason, and selfishness, always seems to mollify our lack of commitment, dedication, and devotion. Therefore, we have become apathetic about our desire to minister unto the Lord. We are left always needing the Lord to minister unto us. Wouldn't it be nice if when we raise our hands to the Lord we do so that the Lord might receive praises? Instead, every time we raise our hands we are surrendering for something we have done wrong or we are asking the Lord to give us something that we define as needful in our lives. To anoint, to sanctify, and to consecrate is to see that person as a very special part of creation. While other men may desire yachts, homes, cars, etc., my desire is that I may be anointed, sanctified, and consecrated, and that all these qualities will appear at one time in my life.

I emphasize "one time" because there are many who will automatically think that if you are anointed, sanctified, or consecrated then you are all three. That is not necessarily the case. They all have different functions. The anointing of the Lord and the sanctification of the Lord are different in that many people who are sanctified have not allowed themselves to access their anointing. Then there are people who have allowed themselves to access the anointing but have not consecrated their whole being unto the Lord. Now you cannot be consecrated without being anointed and sanctified. You cannot be anointed without being sanctified. However, you can be sanctified without being anointed and consecrated, and you can be sanctified and anointed without being consecrated. When you have the composite of all three you are then the choice of God and He entrusts you with ministering substance. Not only does He trust you with these substances, but He also trusts you with the ability to recognize the need in other people's lives and you stand in His stead. (Please, be careful with this statement because the intent is not to suggest idolatry.) Often, the Lord uses us as His angels to help other people to understand His will. Again, I emphasize that standing in God's stead only means standing at the door and taking the tickets while people come in. We must understand that we too have to pay (do our part) for our tickets, which means free access into heaven.

I am so grateful to the Lord for giving me the opportunity to experience His anointing, His sanctification, and His consecration at one time. They have kept me from the laws of con-artistry, from the idea of thinking that I cannot be pure and pristine, and from the mentality that I would have to live a life of chimerical and apocryphal behavior without really knowing if the Lord is pleased with my life. You recognize how big God really is after consecration, and you recognize how "way off" we are, as a human race, in understanding God. It may cause us to question why God seemingly made this thing so perplexing. The answer is that He did not but it takes consecration and an intimate relationship with Him to understand the things that go on.

Imagine a house with eight rooms; four rooms downstairs and four rooms upstairs. One of the rooms upstairs is huge, the master suite as you may know it. That is where God lives.

You knock on the door. God answers through the intercom and invites you to come in. Consider yourself at home.

Now consider another side to this scenario. You roam around in the four rooms downstairs and you come upstairs and roam through three rooms but when you get to God's room the door is locked. You hear Him in there and you hear something going on inside and so you knock on the door. You knock harder and harder and harder but no one seems to respond. All of a sudden the door opens and God asks if He can help you. You respond with a request to enter. He replies, "You cannot come in. You are not prepared to come in here because you are not consecrated." You respond with, "Yes Lord, but you anointed me for your use once, and I am sanctified." God replies, "This may be true, but you are not consecrated and the people that hang around me must worship me in spirit and in truth." This is indicative of God's request upon our lives. He wants us prepared and ready to come into His presence to worship Him, thus ministering unto Him. Our verbal compliments in the presence of God are not as necessary as our submission and surrenderence. In God's presence, eyes are opened, ears are unstopped and tongues are loosened.

An invitation into the presence of God is a major compliment. We are evoked by His very presence to praise Him. However, our praises are so different when we are consecrated. They are not filled with gaps, openings, voids, and emptiness. They are fulfilled. They have direction, destiny, and a sense of purpose, which makes them easy to render. This induces continuous praise until you lose yourself, often falling prostrate before God. Exodus 32:29 reads, "For Moses had said, Consecrate yourselves to day to the Lord… that he may bestow upon you a blessing this day." Bestow means to put to use, to apply, to position, to situate. If Moses' message is as I think it is, then he told the people to consecrate themselves so that the Lord their God could put to use the parts of them that ought to be considered a blessing.

It ought to be a blessing to be used by the Lord except for the scale of judgment when freed from thinking that there are degrees of importance in the Lord's use. Pastors are often considered the "biggest" and the most important part of the church. The Lord may really use them but they are no more important than the stragglers off of the streets if they are not consecrated. That is like the issue of God calling a woman or a man to preach. I pray and hope that all of us have gotten over this stage of competitive ignorance.

For the sake of simplicity, what if the Lord does call a woman to ministry and she is consecrated but he did not call a man and thus he is not consecrated. How do we explain our acceptance of this scenario based on sexuality? Certainly the Lord uses he or she who is consecrated and bestows the blessing of ministry upon him or her. I am so grateful that this blessing does not require a certain sexuality or agenda. We just need devotion and a willingness to surrender to be set apart for the Lord's use. I Chronicles 29:5 asks who is willing to consecrate himself to the Lord, to actually set himself apart, to dedicate and devote himself to the service and worship of God? This means that our personal time may be interrupted. The Lord may come and intercept our idea of pleasure. He may not give us the liberty that we have assumed in life but our reward is consecration, sanctification, and anointing, which gives us the ability to remove yokes from people's necks and burdens from their shoulders. Sanctification gives us significance in society and puts us in a separate and unique category where men will see our good works and glorify our Father, which is in heaven (St. Matthew 5:16).

These are the signs that we ought to be trusting for identification on our spiritual credit report. We should not show the signs of how we deceived, manipulated, and persuaded people using the tunnels of psychological warfare and mind manipulation. There is no consecration in this kind of behavior. When we consider the whole picture, there really is not much of a consecration at all. When we do have this period, it should exemplify a God deserving quality because He is a quality giving God. He deserves our earnestness, honesty, and authenticity. I believe that God requires consecration from all of us.

In Ezekiel 43:26, we read the words, "…and they shall consecrate themselves." There are things that we can do to put ourselves in consecration with the Lord. For example, keep a careful watch of our mode and code of conduct. Make sure that our motives are lined up with the will of God for our lives using the Word of God, the Bible, as our law of principles and governing map. The Lord will consecrate our gain and substance. This means that He will set them apart and dedicate them to make sure that they maintain their status quo. The same is true with our prosperity.

Remember, Jesus mentions that we are His choice in St. John 15:16. He is not our choice. He has ordained us and sent us to bring forth much fruit and that our fruit should remain and be perpetually full and prosperous, "by a new and living way, which he hath consecrated for us, through the veil, that it is to say, his flesh"(Hebrews 10:20). In Numbers 6:7 it reads, "…the consecration of his God is upon his head" (his mind). This means that his mind is filled with the promises of the Lord therefore making him think the thoughts of God, sanctified and holy thoughts filled with dedication, thoughts that are pure, honest, and of a good report. This is the consecration that the Lord requires of our lives.

Now let us examine con-artistry as opposed to consecration to see just how thin the line is between the two. The church has been infiltrated with the spirit of "con-artistry".

A REVERSAL OF ROLES

The one thing that consecration should not be defined as is consecution, which is a chain of reasoning. Consecration demands much more from us than just logic and reason, both of which are usually selfishly based. I really believe that consecration is the Lord's desire for the Christian wardrobe. Con-artistry, in the same light, is the enemy's wardrobe. The divine knowledge of God still leaves me in awe when I settle down and try to think within the framework of His doings. He has never trusted man with His credit. Very few men, if any, will admit to having been carried away at one time or another with the thought of being the Lord's credit carrier, having a feeling of special importance because of something that the Lord used them to perform. This often leads to idolatrous distractions and a loss of focus and concentration, subsequently giving a vague idea on the importance of consecration. Within consecration is a special compliment that should serve to satisfy one's perception of oneself as being insignificant and worthless.

I believe that the greatest virtue is to be set apart for the worship of God. It indicates the Lord's pleasure with your welcomed company. God only allows those who make Him happy into His company. Our consecration is our passport to His divine company and His company of angels. Not everyone is or can be consecrated. Those who are, are first, the choices of God. (What a major compliment!) Consecration is the language of true worship. It automatically equips us for worship. St. John 4:22-24 reads, "Ye worship ye know not what: we know what we worship: for salvation is of the Jews. But the hour cometh, and now is, when the true worshippers shall worship the Father in spirit and in truth: for the Father seeketh such to worship him. God is a

Spirit: and they that worship him must worship him in spirit and in truth."

I believe that Jesus is speaking of the religious contributions in gestures that many church people engage in when they do what is called worship (St. Matthew 15:19). This scripture is used to indicate just how vital the heart is to those who aspire worship. Please consider these scriptures for your advancement in the study of worship: St. John 4:22-24, Acts 17:23, Philippians 3:3, Hebrews 1:6, St. John 9:31, Hebrews 10:2. I truly believe many people worship without even knowing whom they are worshipping. I will give man credit for at least knowing that the Lord exists because He has constantly heard His name being called. However, this is not enough. It is impossible to know God unless we spend time with Him. Our consecration is decided by our knowledge and involved application of His intimate character. I truly believe that more people would love to be intimate with the Lord but the requirements are so compelling to the flesh person, who has not denied himself, taken up his cross and followed Christ (St. Matthew 16:24). It is very perplexing to me why we have settled for not knowing Him in an intimate way.

Con is the tool of the game. Artistry is the charisma used to gain advantage. For years, people have mastered fooling other folks. Many get joy from the success of this wicked art. The church world is filled with these games and cons. I have seen people do what is called laying hands on others. This is often done with a hand tremble that usually indicates that the recipient should shake also. There are several procedures used in this kind of con-ministry: the "slap upside the head," the oily hand, the push the head back, the back bender, the push, the bend down, and many more. This may seem a little hilarious but it is true. Many altar calls precede con-games.

Many of these con-games will precede a request for money. The consecration leaves when the con-games starts.

We are quick to show "cutaways" of what we call "being slain in the spirit" (in television, cutaways are when the editor, in brief intervals, shows the audience as opposed to the speaker). I really question the act and the words. Many times it is only a physical gesture of an emotional moment. If a man tries to use the Bible to defend this very possible con-game procedure, he will not find it advantageous in a debate with someone else who reads the Bible as well. What really goes on at these times? Would you please tell the truth? Most people fall, "slammed" because they think that is what they are supposed to do. The laying on of hands is supposed to signify agreement and not induce physical activity, although this may accompany agreement. It is not to suggest, "fall" to the individual. In some cases, the person may lay for long periods of time constantly blinking trying to keep the light out of their eyes. This is not a mockery of the prayer lines we have, however I have not chosen to defend my point of view with people who acclaim to know and love truth.

I believe that the truth makes us free (St. John 8:32). While everyone may not be guilty of this con-game, many are. I would rather jeopardize my friendship with the few that are not, if they do not yield to understand, than to sit back as an apostle and do nothing about these con-games. This will make anyone who uses this procedure uncomfortable unless they admit that in some situations this is the case. Many people are told to give money during these emotional times, and with the help of a will to please the Lord and trust in the one asking, they obey what is asked of them.

I personally have had times when the Spirit so overshadowed me that I became weak in my knees. I have received visions and have fallen prostrate before the Lord God without the help of someone's push or pull. Many of you have perhaps had a similar experience as well. Then, there are many that have faked falling and faked being anointed when they have prayed for others and this must stop. This is not the Lord. It is only credence and it is usually done during a time that can be defined as consecration. My what a thin line!

Another con-game is the "blowing in your face" game, suggesting that an impartation of the Holy Spirit is being given. While many of my friends will frown at me for this, I know that their love for the Lord will direct them to at least research what I have written and prove to themselves that what they do is unspiritual and incorrect. No one should use the phrases "I know what God told me," or "you don't know what God told me" as a defense. I say this because every man who is a leader will have someone to follow if he is right or wrong. Most of our close associates will not share with us what they really think for fear of losing our friendship. Thus, we should never accept the permission of close associates as God's permission.

When I started writing I vowed to be honest, truthful, and not given to others' opinions and ideas about my candid conversation. I know the feeling that comes with knowing you are faking but going through with it anyway. That is why I write as I do. I was trapped one day. I was asked to pray for people during one of my most unspiritual times. I was not anointed that day. I thank the Lord, the people were. They had access to the Lord's presence; I didn't. I played the role. I am ashamed of that act in my past and will never allow it to take place again. However, I must confess that it did happen. I developed an understanding of this con-game ministry through that experience. The people thought I was consecrated and anointed but I was not. My only access was the "know how" of the ministry. I remember wanting the people to fall and pushing back on their heads so that they would. Most of all, I remember going home that night ashamed, scared and despondent that I had stooped so low. I had fooled some but angered the Lord.

The men and women of God will applaud my boldness and unintended arrogance. A con-artist will accuse me of attacking preachers and calling them con-artists. It is strange. I could call these same people astronauts and it would not faze them but when I speak or write on the subject of con-artistry it agitates them. I wonder why? It does not imply unless it applies.

Preachers are very sensitive. I once had a person in my life that called himself my friend. We would exchange fellowship by going to lunch, laughing together, telling a few jokes (those of you who are "jokeless" forgive me), and even share secrets. One day I was asked to come and speak on his behalf. I changed my schedule to do so. I ministered on a Saturday night and gave a generous offering. I even expressed offense at the idea of his administration wanting to reward me with an honorarium. Honorariums are in order and I advocate them. It was his special anniversary and I thought that it would be inappropriate to take money that had been raised for him. I felt good that I had this kind of character and integrity, to God be the glory.

There are many preachers who con the people to give a lot to the pastor in order to boost the honorarium. I kid you not. Visiting pastors and host pastors are often in agreement with con-games where money is concerned. If you think I am kidding ask the Lord and then open your eyes during the offering ministry and you will see what I am saying.

Let us get back to the story, which will be an admonishment to reciprocity. This same gesture did not work to my advantage during my anniversary. (Forgive me, those of you who do not believe in anniversaries, etc.) The date was approaching and my administrator asked my friend to speak on my behalf. To our surprise we were told that it would cost us. Yes, he who I did not charge was now charging me. This may sound like I am getting things off of my chest or that I am throwing a stone, quite the contrary. I wish to make a point about con-artistry and without implying that my friend is a con-artist. If the Lord is in what we do then He will and shall rule. Unfortunately, our friendship was broken and our possible future fellowship on the line due to our discussion of this matter and my reproving what I thought was an unethical action. Before you express your "oooos" and "ahhhhhs," let me say that there is hardly a church that does not have some other church that it will not fellowship with because of bias, prejudice, or maybe denominational reasons. Some may even have money as the reason. The con-game is that the enemy persuaded this man of God to stoop to an economical principle that exceeded his character and integrity to not fellowship with someone who was proven faithful through the years. The con gets greater. His position was explained and selfishly justified so eloquently that he probably will never understand his error.

True prosperity is being replaced by con games. The tool that is needed to continue in these con games is someone else's opinion and agreement. The greatest con, I believe, is against our character as pastors. The enemy will promise us something while blinding us with how much we are losing. We will never lose if we stick to our initial character that was sanctified and aspiring holiness. Unfortunately, our pride and arrogance will not allow us to do so when we defend wrong. Leaders will usually teach what they themselves do, be it right or wrong. This is another form of being conned because we must give an account for what we do. Too many people are following con-artists while trying to teach others to follow Christ. This is a hard thing to do and someone is going to lose. The con-game will not leave room for consecration. We can only get worse unless we repent of our ways.

To all leaders, the message of this chapter is "don't sell out." Keep a spiritual standard. Most of all please watch who you hang with. Life is contagious and I am not sure if you can resist. Some world examples of con-games include lying, distrust, intent to deceive, hypocrisy, smiling, and generosity. Compare them to the information I have just shared and you should concur that there is a *thin line between consecration and con-artistry*.

PREACHING OR PIMPING

I remember when this new age, contemporary, secular humanistic, prosperity teaching started filling the church atmosphere. I would hear different ones saying things that I knew were the beginning of a change-over in the church world. This was all based on a scripture that was taken totally out of context, "Behold, I will do a new thing; now it shall spring forth; shall ye not know it? I will even make a way in the wilderness, and rivers in the desert" (Isaiah 43:19).

I wish to address a situation that occurred between me and an old acquaintance of mine: *We were both shopping independently in the mall when we noticed each other, embraced, greeted, and savored the past. She asked me how my ministry was doing. I remember saying, "Well I'm pastoring 'our people.' You know how that can be." I did not intend to sound stereotypical, although I may have been. I was just having conversation. Then I turned the tables on her. I asked, "So, how are things with you?" The answer I received was as much a concern as it was a travesty. She told me that she had left her church. I was almost afraid to ask her why because the answer may have grown to be painful. There was nothing in the world, I thought, that could ever make this person leave the church she had attended all of her life. She was a member of a Baptist church, dedicated, devoted, and very respectful to her leader. Her reply to me was, "I had to get away from all of that preaching, jumping, and squalling. I had to find me some teaching." I knew her pastor and while he was not eloquent and enticing with words, he loved the Lord and was honest. I needed clarification about her response. She continued by saying she had joined a "Word Church." To my chagrin I replied, "A Word Church! What is a Word Church?" She replied, "You know, a teaching ministry where they teach the Word."*

She kept talking. Her excitement became borderline rude. She stated firmly, "I was tired of hearing about the three Hebrew boys and Daniel in the lion's den. I needed teaching so I left that dead church and joined this church and I have done nothing but prospered since I've been there. I have a new car, a better job, and I have not looked back." My heart pained, first for the pastor who I knew at least loved her, and then for the young lady and all whom she meets and shares this terrible testimony of changing churches.

Many people have jumped from the frying pan into the fire thinking that they have gained the advantage. Unfortunately much of this is done through mind manipulation. Mind manipulation, and its influences, has been around for some years. It has become stronger and more dangerous since contemporary and spiritual cultures started intermingling with one another. I advocate and endorse fellowship but not at the expense of mind control. (Please be open-minded when you read this section.)

Another problem we have in the body of Christ is our ability to hear another's opinion without taking it as a personal attack. Those who are of the Pentecostal background have forever been an emotional group. We praise and worship God in our own way with a delivery that is stylish and demonstrative, and even flamboyant at times. Many of our practices were attacked and mocked as stupid, senseless, and out of order. Our clichés were mimicked and our songs called doubt-filled. For instance, the old song where the deacon would kneel at the chair and begin lamenting, *"This may be the last time, this may be the last time, this may be the last time, it may be the last time, I don't know,"* is now mimicked as an ignorant song. The motive for this mockery is to belittle those to whom the song is meaningful and to manipulate the manner in which they think.

The theory behind the songs origin is that, during the days of slavery it was nothing for a slave master to come into the slave quarters and get a slave for the purpose of being an example. That slave may have been found the next day hanging from a tree, stretched out over a fire, etc. So, when a slave was taken from his quarters in the dark, as a prayer the others would all kneel and sing, *"This may be the last time, this may be the last time, this may be the last time, I don't know."* They did not know if the person would ever return. This is a fraction of history that explains some of the actions of our culture.

If I wanted to trick people into following me, I would probably use the strategies of "divide and conquer" to do so. I would make them think that what they were doing and what they have learned is totally ignorant. I would tell them how much they have lost by being at their present church and I would convince them that they should come over to where I am to learn what I want to teach them. I would fill their minds with the thoughts of their innate desires and then create a fear of loss within them, (the oldest sales trick there is). Then, I would tell them to pray about it because I would not want them to leave their church. It would be too late. They have been manipulated to think that their foundation is not good for them and at best, it was only good enough to bring them to this point in their lives.

This strategy is often used not only inside ones culture but it is commonly used to divide specific races against their own cultural beliefs. What happens is that one culture teaches another culture to blame their foundation. I cannot believe that the Black race has accepted the lie that our songs are demeaning, ignorant, and not Word oriented. Where did all of this come from?

I'm Climbing Up The Rough Side Of The Mountain was described as pathetic with a stupid confession. The truth is the song speaks of a reality. The strength is in the fact that, at least, I am climbing up, and I haven't stopped. Also it speaks of the reality of life's rough side. I am not sitting and pouting because of the roughness of the mountains in life.

I was embarrassed one wintry day, when someone who was once a member of my church said to me after I sneezed, "Pastor, rebuke the devil. Don't claim that thing." I was appalled at the teaching he had received in thinking that a common cold, brought on by my irresponsible neglect to wear proper clothing, was caused by the devil. When are we going to accept the fact that Christians are dying from diseases every day? Pastors, who preach faith and healing, are suffering with prostate cancer, kidney failure, high blood pressure, AIDS and many more diseases. A young preacher, who still works out, may think that he is exempt from diseases, but if you check the record, it would indicate that all of us will die from something, unless of course the Lord's return catches us first.

I am afraid that all we have done is confused the issue, torn up churches, and broken relationships between pastors and members. Calling ourselves Word Churches should not be enough to deceitfully convince people to leave their foundation. However, at times this has been proven to be enough. I do not advocate that anyone should die in an unspiritual state. We should make sure that our motives lie in the Word of God and not in prosperity. I am almost convinced that the ideology of prosperity is often the true reasons for changing churches.

Preaching is a part of church. It has always been and it will always be. I would really like to know how teaching became a better tool for church growth than preaching. In my opinion, they both need each other. The most important need is for individuals to read for themselves. Study God's Word in private so that no one can preach you into apathy or seduce you into propaganda and pragmatism. In Jonah 3:2, Jonah is given an assignment to preach to the city the message that God bid he preach. John the Baptist, the forerunner of Jesus Christ our Lord, expresses his ministry in preaching (St. Matthew 3:1). St. Matthew 4:23 reads, "And Jesus went about all Galilee, teaching in their synagogues, and preaching the gospel of the kingdom…." Here is an occasion where Jesus did both; He preached and taught. Also, St. Matthew 12:41 states, "The men of Nineveh shall rise in judgment with this generation, and shall condemn it: because they repented at the preaching of Jonas; and, behold, a greater than Jonas is here." Here is an occasion where preaching saved a city. In Acts 8:4 it reads, "Therefore they that were scattered abroad went everywhere preaching the word." Please do not try to slip in the hidden Greek meaning because the Greek definition would have taught us not to build our church on another man's foundation.

Most of Paul's teachings were conveyed in a preaching manner. Exactly what do people mean when they say a teaching ministry as opposed to a preaching ministry? Please be on the lookout for perpetrators who advocate teaching above preaching. Ask them for a sound reason for their position. In Romans 10:14 it reads, "How then shall they call on him in whom they have not believed? and how shall they believe in him of whom they have not heard? and how shall they hear without a preacher?"

PREACH

Lexical Aids to the New Testament, pages 928 and 2784, gives the Greek word for preach: Kêrussô; to preach, herald, proclaim (St. Matthew 3:1; St. Mark 1:45; St. Luke 4:18, 19; 12:3; Acts 10:37; Romans 2:21; Revelation 5:2). In 1 Peter 3:19, there is no reference to evangelizing, but rather to the act of Christ, after His resurrection, in proclaiming His victory to fallen spirits. To preach the gospel as a herald (St. Matthew 24:14; St. Mark 13:10; 14:9; 16:15, 20; St. Luke 8:1; 9:2; 24:47; Acts 8:5; 19:13; 28:31; Romans 10:14); to preach the Word (2 Timothy 4:2). Deriv.: prokêrússô (4296), from pro (4253), before, and kêrússô, to proclaim before or ahead (Acts 3:20 TR; 13:24); kêrugma (2782), a proclamation by a herald, denotes preaching, the substance of which is distinct from the act of preaching; kêrux (2783), a herald, used of the preacher of the gospel (1 Timothy 2:7; 2 Timothy 1:11), and of Noah as a preacher of righteousness (2 Peter 2:5).

TEACH

Lexical Aids to the New Testament, pages 933 and 3100, gives the Greek word for teach: Mathêteúô; from mathêtês (3101), disciple. Governing a dat., to be a disciple or follower of another's doctrine (St. Matthew 27:57); governing an acc., to make a disciple (St. Matthew 28:19; Acts 14:21); to instruct (St. Matthew 13:52) with the purpose of making a disciple Mathêteúô means not only to learn but to become attached to one's teacher and to become his follower in doctrine and conduct. It is really not sufficient to translate this verb as "learn" but as "making a disciple" in its trans. Meaning, in the NT sense of mathêtês. Deriv.: manthánô (3129), to cause oneself to know.

We should be very careful who we give the right to transfer knowledge, especially when it is based on their ulterior motive to gain members into their own fold. The word teach, mathêteúô, also suggests an attachment to the teacher. (Please be careful.) It is misleading if we believe that preaching is not good for learning. It is as important for us to receive preaching as it is teaching. However, the most important thing is that we study for ourselves.

Much of what we call teaching, is really a pathway for pimping. Think about it. A person can persuade you to leave your foundation and follow him. He then persuades you to believe in a doctrine that is not biblically sound such as tongue speaking without interpretation, which I believe is being taught in error. Many people were made to do what is called "speaking in tongues." They were taken to special rooms and the elders laid hands on them until they did something called speaking gibberish surnamed speaking in tongues. Many were given words to say and then told "that's it, you've done it." They were hypocritical, saying they did speak when they knew that they did not. We are prime candidates for being pimped. Most of these ministries are geared toward unsound people, intending to build an empire with those who are given to every wind of doctrine. They are masters at getting us to see and believe in "A" and "B" that is right, so they can deceive us with "C," which is erroneous.

There is a very *thin line between pimping and preaching.* When you are told that you must perform a service of giving in order to prosper, you are being pimped. When you find a church that promises to help you stay spiritual after you have left your former church, promises you spiritual food that is better than preaching (through the vehicle of teaching), and tells that you are the head and not the tail as long as you are a part of their ministry, then you are being pimped.

It is not an easy task writing this book in which much truth is shared. Although truth is designed to give us an opportunity for freedom, it too easily makes us uncomfortable. The word of God tells us in St. Matthew 5:6 that we are blessed in proportion to our hunger for righteousness. Again, I wish to emphasize the fact that there is *a thin line between preaching and pimping.*

PIMPING OR PREACHING

Pimping along with prostitution is one of the world's oldest professions. It is really nothing more than living off the earnings of another person. It is unspiritual and wrong. It is illegal in many cases. Pro-prostitution movements propose to decriminalize pimping so that the pimps can be treated as helpers and/or companions. Once a person's mind has been pimped or manipulated he has also been raped of his right of judgment from then on. Subsequently he is prone to placing all pastors in a category of being a pimp. This is the travesty of the ministry.

Pimping is a condition of slavery while being promised freedom and satisfaction. Many of our leaders have turned into pure pimps under the pretense of being a preacher. You will have to judge this matter for yourself. My job is to share truth with you. Your job is to eat or not to eat that truth. This slave-minded position can be found in situations where people have made their leaders gods.

The most frightening day of my life was when a young parishioner said, "Pastor, I did not know that you could catch a cold," after hearing me sneeze. This young mind thought that I was so spiritual that I, superceded natural laws. I tremble at the idea of someone thinking that I am like a god. That is farthest from the truth. However, this could have been a great opportunity for me to tell her, "I am pretty close to God and He told me to tell you to give your full pay check to me and you will be blessed." She would have done so, and only God knows what else. Instead, I saw a young lady in trouble in her mind via the lack of knowledge. I immediately started on a mission to rescue her from her gullibility. Thank God I was successful in doing so, with the help of many of my staff members. Needless to say, it happened to her again a few years later. This time she would not allow the staff to help her. She fell into the arms of a pimp that seduced her. First, he promised her liberty from the bondage she was in as it related to going to church. He broke her spirit, took away the bridge to return home, showed her the beauty of the world, and then closed the door and began deforming her mind.

First, he made her think that the good people around her were bad for her. (This is what I am afraid may happen with this book. Many will be encouraged not to read it. Truth is all that it is.) Secondly, he started asking her to do things for him that would give him the advantage in her life. Reluctantly, she did what she was asked and eventually those things became laws by which she lived. I can understand how this trickery can happen to a "church person." My concerns go much deeper to include many of my peers who have vowed to preach the truth in season (II Timothy 4:2).

Listen to the truth in a parable:

A man receives a calling from the Lord to preach. He starts off doing just fine but he is not making a lot of money. One particular evening he goes to dinner with a friend of his who has been preaching for years. When asked how the ministry is doing, in his youthfulness he answers, "Not very good because we can barely pay our bills and I get very little for my services." Silence reigns for a moment, then the elder states. "Your problem is you are not teaching them the power of seed sowing. You are not forming the money lines. You are not manipulating their giving." A trembling reply comes from the confused young preacher. He thought that his job was to preach and not to pimp. When he considered the elder's success and growth in membership, he was forced to believe that his friend might have known what he was talking about.

The facts were he had a huge church, which he thought meant a lot of members on roll, an airplane in which he traveled all over the world, and renownedness.

The young preacher's reply, founded on curiosity rather than integrity. "How do you get the people to give when you preach against their sins?" The elder replies with an asinine smile on his face, "I don't. That's no longer my concern. I see it like this. It's between them and the Lord. As long as they give up the money, they can commit adultery, fornicate, and even practice homosexuality. I'm not going to touch it and risk the chance of losing all of those good tithe payers."

The young man appears disappointed and borderline angry. He replies in this fashion, "I think I'll stay as I am and keep preaching the pure gospel, which sometimes interferes with having a comfortable lifestyle. My desire to face the Lord free of guilt is greater than that of gaining material things. My title is not as glamorous as yours. I'm not a bishop, apostle, etc., I'm just a pastor. I'm just a little preacher. I will say this, 'I had rather be a doorkeeper in the house of my God, than to dwell in the tents of wickedness.'" He rises, grabs his ticket, leaves his tip and keeps his character.

Leaders must take a stand if they are to maintain their character. The people of God are precious to God. The Lord entrusted us with their lives and told us to lead them after the example of Jesus. Today, many choose to pimp the people of God, count them as you would livestock, and put a price tag on them to ensure that the financial goals of the services are met. Pimping begins in the prayer lines. Leaders prostitute God's people, asking them to perform services for rewards. The expected service is that the people promote the prostitute and the pimp as having some special godly power. The reward to the people is a word of prophecy. In others words, market the man instead of the Lord. Also I would like to warn my readers that they are being pimped when they pay for a word of prophecy.

A brochure from a conference read, "Everyone who pays $40 will receive a prophetic word and will be prayed for." A friend of mine told me of his going to a certain prophet for advice and paying him thousands for his answers to the "Dow Jones Average." As previously stated, the devil will give you "A" and "B" that is right, so he can get you to believe "C" that is wrong.

One young lady, just delivered from an occult, when asked how she gained such confidence in the leader, she replied, "Because of his ability to tell people about their lives." Later on in the conversation she did admit that he missed sometimes.

In almost every church, the people who make the most money, especially when you start targeting those in the millionaire status, are the least givers based on percentage. However, their least in giving is still much more than most people's most. This should not give them the right to rob God.

We should also remember that the pimp always feels a "right" to all of the people working for him. The *thin line between pimping and preaching* is indicated as we observe the invitation list to the pastor's home. The millionaire or politician is always welcomed. Everyone else must call first. Oh, let me ask this, why isn't the leader's phone number accessible? I wonder why this is so? While some things are common to understand, we must be careful of the hypocrisy portrayed when we invite one thing and leave out the other.

A pimp promises to protect while failing to tell you what God's will is for your life, as it relates to sin. Remember a pimp's only love is money. I have watched movies where the pimp promises to love and protect his workers, until they mess with his money. A pimp wants his workers to dress enticingly to draw clients. I am not sure if this is not what we are doing when we advocate a lack of dress code in our services: come as you are. I will not mess with your mini-skirts if you tithe and allow me to pimp your money. Isn't this what spiritual leaders are saying?

When it was noised abroad that I was going into the television ministry, I received so much advice on what I should and should not preach. While good advice is appreciated, I must be careful and make sure that the motive is not based on someone's idea of preaching relative to prosperity and gain. What do people mean when they say you should not preach doctrine? Every church preaches doctrine. Most churches have their own dogma. An outsider can define almost all churches' beliefs as doctrine.

The *thin line between pimping and preaching* gets thinner when a "service" instead of a worship service is the focal point. If I take you in as a member, promise to feed you the unadulterated Word of God, and then use you to make money for the church, I am a pimp. If you are just a number to me then I could very easily be a pimp to you. Most of what we hear as "God told me to do this or that" is exactly the opposite. It is not fair to the people of God when the leader-turned-pimp keeps having visions that induce territorial growth at the expense of the Word of God. There are still some good "Word of God" preachers left. However they are very hard to find. Many preachers have sold out to the cliques and fraternities of the pulpit.

When I kiss the elderly mothers of the church, making them believe that they are important, when in actuality, all I care about is having their insurance policies in my name when they die, I am a pimp. Also, they are the "adhesive" that keeps the rest of their family in church.

Many people who are tricked by mind control and psychological warfare will not realize, until it is too late, that they have been pimped. It has been my opinion that this realization may leave one angry, disillusioned, and vindictive without a basis for choosing in the future, independent of the reminder of the past. Paranoia sets in and everyone from then on is suspect. The tragedy from this travesty is the knowledge that is now rejected because of what happened in the past.

Categories make all of us suspect. For instance, there was a Jim who coerced many people to drink cyanide poison. Then, there was a Jim accused in the PTL scandal. Another Jim was allegedly caught spending time with a prostitute. I have been called Jim often, although my name is James. I stand vulnerable to falling because I am not perfect. I gain speed in my concerns when I hear these kinds of statements, "Ain't non of dem prechees kno gudd. On'd trus non abein had name stard wit J." (Ain't none of them preachers no good. I don't trust none of them with the name that starts with "J.") I truly thank God that the name of Jesus starts with a "J." Now this is a category in which I do not mind being classified. Jesus was totally against the idea of pimping and unjustly living off the earnings of others.

The one reason we must protect our minds against infiltration is because of the future detriment to our relationship with others, and most importantly with the Lord. It is very hard for someone in a bad marriage to birth encouragement about the institution of marriage. A bad marriage should teach the lesson of carefulness and watchfulness, which are good to exercise. Over the years, I have noticed just how easy it is to overlook this negative experience as nothing but a "thang" when a new interest in marriage resurfaces. It is almost as if the past did not happen. I am not suggesting that we should be paranoid, but I firmly advocate that we spend a little more time talking with the Lord and a little less time talking with people.

In this section, my goal is to teach you independence thus removing you from the power of pimping. Preaching, like pimping, can be rape and kidnapping, which are equal to other systematic practices as forms of mind control. Hundreds of workers have reported being raped by their pimps. Thousands have reported working for the pastor who was the only one that profited. When a pastor preaches to people that they must tithe and he does not, he has become a hypocrite and a pimp. **MANY PASTORS DO NOT TITHE. CHECK THE RECORDS. PLEASE CHECK THE RECORDS. PIMPS DO NOT PAY TAXES. MANY PREACHERS DO NOT PAY TAXES, THEREFORE LEAVING THE CHURCH INSECURE.** The leader should have his act together. There is *a thin line between pimping and preaching.*

A pimp's message to a prostitute is to go out and bring in the money. I will dress up and array myself in prosperity. I will look good when you get back. Many talented and gifted people are being pimped for those qualities. When your contribution is based on your worth and or significance, then you are being pimped. Everyone has a soul, which should be the primary interest of the leader's relationship with the individual. For instance, a musician is fired. His tenure as a church employee has ended, not his church membership. However, because this is not the case, he is also encouraged to leave the church. Service should never be just a job.

I believe that we have started a war that will cause many souls to be lost, when we pay people to use the Lord's talents in a service dedicated to God. Unfortunately, this is usually the case with drummers, musicians, etc. There is little continuity in service when money and business dictate tenure. Ultimately, this will cause a clash of venue. These conditions are not illusive and these writings are not merely rhetorical. Church should be a place of worship and not a slave camp where members "do what I, the leader, say and not as I do."

Slavery is an objective social condition that requires escape in order for the victim to get out. All slave masters were pimps. Any pastor teaching prosperity above purity will put the minds of the people of God in bondage and he has become a pimp. This is one aspect of the violation that goes on from our pulpits. There are some forms of prostitution that are not pimp-controlled. Hopefully, we can deal with these issues in a future book.

Mind manipulation is hard to stop once it gets started. There are two chains that need to be broken in relation to being pimped. The first is verbal thus psychological. Giving ear to teaching without conducting personal research is very dangerous. 90% of what we believe and repeat is probably not researched. When you are told that you will not prosper if you do not submit to what someone says, then you are being manipulated into mind control, this is done possibly through the tunnel of ambiguity.

The second chain is the chain of fear, the creation of the sense of loss. This may happen by the exploitation of testimonies relating to the same subject. A testimony should be to the glory of the Lord but this is not always the case. Many times it is for marketing reasons first. A pimp wants to control the mind more than the body. It does not take a rocket scientist to figure this strategy out. The body goes and does what the mind tells it. The Lord requires love, loyalty and obedience as well as self-discipline. The intent of the new fad in contemporary teaching based on pragmatic principles and secular humanism is to create a different environment. It is a brainwashing process. It is all about interesting creativity. Many fraudulent acts are taking place from the pulpit. It may be time to take on a new identity and start the arduous and enormous task of putting your life back together.

Spiritual suicide can be inevitable from this kind of mind control. We are not prostitutes and products of pimping. We are the children of God and deserve to know the truth. This book is our life raft, our safety plane. Enjoy this truth and let it make you free. "And ye shall know the truth, and the truth shall make you free" (St. John 8:32). This monster of mind manipulation has no gender, race, creed, or color that it will not affect if allowed to. The philosophy is very simple. The pimp runs everything, according to his own will. He offers the members a contract by way of covenant-type teachings. This contract reads, "You are joining this church because you have passed one of the requirements in becoming a member of this illustrious family. You have left traditionalism and have joined human secularism and pragmatism. This life is just like a large-scale movie production with myself as the producer and you as the star. The world is your audience and the entire universe is your stage. Enjoy your stay with us."

People who are naïve, lonely, bitter, and rebellious are prime candidates for being trapped by mind control. There are simply too many people out in the world without a commitment to a church or ministry. This is not the Lord's will for His sheep. All sheep should have a shepherd. You do not become a shepherd just because you have a bad experience as a sheep. Many so-called pastors are really nothing more than failed "sheep" without the humility to admit it.

Please remember that anyone can always get someone to follow him. If you could operate on the hearts of your sheep you, no doubt, would find true feelings that admit to your non-authenticity. You do not become a leader just because you failed at being a follower. Every person should be careful when going through a stage of resistance, prudishness or being scared because they may also be vulnerable to the same.

There are all kinds of manipulations taking place such as pouting preachers, who threaten to leave the church if "x" amount of dollars are not raised. Climbing towers and pouting unless millions of dollars are received is not uncommon. A pastor's denial of possessing pimp qualities becomes a way of expressing that his own experience does not coincide with the stereotypical pimp and prostitute relationship. I am convinced that there is *a thin line between pimping and preaching* when we consider all the factors.

Please make sure that what you do is done with God as the focus, for only then will you never be pimped by man. Man may think that he is pimping you but your deeds of giving and sharing are recorded in heaven and you will be rewarded from the same.

ANOINTING OR ANARCHY

Anarchy

1. Absent of spiritual government.
2. A state of lawlessness due to the absence of governmental authority.
3. A society having no government and is made up of individuals who enjoy complete freedom.
4. The absence of a master and the rule of law.

Anointing

1. God's placement of His nature in its total essence with destiny as its purpose and victory as its goal. (Apostle James S. Prothro)
2. The ordination of God's will in complete security.
3. Blessing joining the team of ordination and promise.

The dictionary's definition of anointing will not do justice in understanding this chapter. However, I will share it with you for the sake of fairness.

4. To rub over with oil (this to me is the act of anointing). To apply or pour oil upon as a sacred rite especially for consecration.

In this world, it is very common to hear of people who believe that there is nothing wrong with anarchy. This is based on relativism, pragmatism, and secular humanism. There are several beliefs about anarchy, which are all classic examples of pure ignorance. To address this issue is to suggest that it must stop. As a matter of fact, this belief suggests that anarchy is the best form of government. In a state of anarchy there is no organized government and the people are their own authority. Not only is there no government but also there is no military competition, no police state, and no terror. In my opinion, this idea is ridiculous. This belief is based on the fact that if there is anarchy then it should be determined by education. I wonder what we would use to govern our teaching principles? We are already aware of what this society and its educational efforts give to spirituality, very little if anything.

I hope to shed light on the fact that there is a thin line between anarchy and what we call anointing. Unfortunately, God's anointing, which should be governmentally controlled by Him and His divine order, has now been given definition and recognition that suggests the absence of not only spiritual government but also spiritual rule. Our society will not demand their that spiritual leaders possess a true anointing. With Darwinism dying a slow death, scientists are being convinced daily and more and more that it is scientifically impossible that there is any credence to the theory of Darwinism. We must not consider ourselves victorious until we have cleaned up the entities that may have been birthed from this kind of worldly ignorance.

Defining *Anarchism*

Anarchism has been defined many ways by many different sources. The word anarchism is taken from the word anarchy, which is drawn from dual sources in the Greek language. It is made up of the Greek words av, which means an absence of (pronounced "an") and apxn, which means authority or government (pronounced "arkhe"). The dictionary defines anarchism as the absence of government. Many pro-anarchists believe that these modern dictionary definitions of anarchism are based on the writings and actions of present and past anarchists. Some anarchists understand and believe that historians of anarchism and good dictionaries and encyclopedias believe that the word anarchism represents a positive theory. Their defense is that exterior sources, such as the media, will frequently misuse the word anarchism and thus breed misunderstanding. While I agree that the media is a satanic tool if used inappropriately, and many times it is, I do not agree with the unspiritual anarchists that anarchy is a positive theory as it relates to the message of this book.

A leading modern dictionary, Webster's Third International Dictionary, defines anarchism briefly but accurately (even the word accurately should be carefully used if you exclude the spiritual need of our society). It reads that anarchism is a politically safe theory opposed to all forms of government and governmental restraint and advocating voluntary cooperation and free association of individuals and groups in order to satisfy their needs (a word used out of context in relation to the Bible). It is also defined as the political doctrine that all governments should be abolished. These similar dictionary definitions reflect the evolution of the theory of anarchism made possible by anarchistic intellectuals and movements. As a result, these definitions, although fair, only reflect watered down definitions of the word anarchism. If anarchism takes over, then church, as we know it is over. Slowly but surely it is happening anyway.

The Word of God is now used to induce self-confidence as a primary achievement. Then, one may choose to add the Lord to the agenda. Have we so quickly forgotten or do we choose not to remember for fear of this knowledge and responsibility, that God rules this world? All else is His choice. He is in control. The Lord never intended for our societies to be free of government. This is proven in Genesis when rules, contingencies, and conditions were given to Adam (Genesis 2:16-17). It was the idea of anarchy that convinced Eve, through the serpent, to appreciate the ideology of lack of government. The serpent suggested, through psychological warfare, that she seek anarchy because God was trying to rule everything (Genesis 3:5). This idea was preached by a misrepresentation of the truth, a blatant and intending to deceive lie. It was also the ultimate of idolatry and emulation. The Lord God's words were, "... thou shalt surely die" (Genesis 2:17). The serpent changed them to, "...ye shall not surely die." The adverb "not," which is used as a function word to make negative a word or group of words, may appear as just a little nuance or even a minor difference. However, it was exactly the opposite of what the Lord God said. It was a lie from a liar about the security of mankind. The suggestion that is implied in the relative text verses is very clear and simple; you do not need to be ruled by the Lord God but you need to be equal to Him. What a travesty! What a trap!

A choice means having resistance to what God chooses. Please be mindful of the facts that God's choice rules our choices. We are only free to choose as God has chosen. "Ye have not chosen me, but I have chosen you..."(St. John 15:16). It is not possible for our "choices" to have freedom. The "chooser" governs them. Only then can our choices have significance. Before, they were only options without probability of use. (I pray that God will lend understanding from the level in which this is written.) Anarchy makes us believe that we have separate freedom within the fact of our being chosen. Even if this is the position of pro-anarchists, we all should concur that a choice is imprisoned and governed by its "chooser," therefore making government not only necessary but also inevitable. In other words, we cannot get around going through the Lord God as our governor. The Word says that the foundation of our leader stands on the fact that he is our government (Isaiah 9:6-7).

Let us consider the definition for the word *choice*: a person or thing that is chosen, a variety of persons or things from which is chosen or may be used to express contingency, especially in clauses indicating conditioning results. Although the word may give permission to choose, it gets its authority from choice (Isaiah 43:7; St John 15:16; II Timothy 1:9). Jesus is the perfect example of how to allow government in one's life and survive. Anarchy will inevitably lead to chaos. We subtly denounce God's absoluteness because of relativism. It is in His absoluteness that we have access to His anointing. He could not and did not trust man to rule himself. For those pro "free moral agent" believers who definitely declare the first state of man to be free moral agency, let me remind you that man was locked into a proximity and governed by the laws of that vicinity. When an enticing opportunity to enter into anarchy seemingly appeared, we saw that it almost cost man his existence (the same for our Jesus' death, burial and resurrection). It did cost man his perpetual reign in the garden of eternal life.

My heart really aches and trembles at the liberty taken by our pastors and leaders about the anointing of God. It is being misused, misconstrued, and abused. It seems as if every time someone wishes to mollify his sacerdotal rights, whether right or wrong, it has become a common practice to suggest that it is taking place by virtue of God's anointing. We have given the anointing a job description that I am sure makes the Lord sick. For instance, I have heard the phrase "I am anointed to take up offering," which is a slick way of saying that one is good at manipulating people to give, or that one is the prostitute used by the pimps to bring in the money. Unfortunately, it does not usually appear distasteful because of the reciprocating reward. In other words, the deal is already contracted at 50/50. How can we allow ourselves to think that the word "anoint" or "anointing" can be used on such a secular level? I pray that the Lord will forgive us for this foolishness, which I believe is irreverence and sinful.

Another misuse of the word *anoint* is when we refer to ourselves as being "anointed to prosper." This statement should go without saying unless it is being used to manipulate others. In this case it is used out of context. The anointing of God is not a substance that we can use to aid in prosperity. The true responsibility of the anointing is to protect the promises of God. We are prosperous because the Lord has ordained us to be and not because we can create strategies to aid us in becoming prosperous.

In the book of Genesis, it was in the Garden of Eden where the serpent insinuated that Eve should be free from God's rule, free to do her own thing and free to roam around in the arena of the knowledge of good and evil. Have you ever considered why the knowledge of evil was so important to her? The Bible verifies that we are responsible for what we know (St. John 4:17). In hindsight, which is foresight too late, she should have interpreted the serpent's association as being pro-anarchism. He promised her freedom but left her in bondage.

In William Godwin's book, *Political Justice,* written in 1793, there are acclaims to the true introduction of the word *anarchy*, this teaching defied the realization of a world that is ruled first by God. God gave man dominion (Genesis 1:28).

In my opinion, the word *dominion* is not limited to power and authority to rule, but it is also government in order. Anarchism became more than just a rejection of established authority when Godwin's book started traveling across the world. It was presented as a theory that opposed ownership of land and property as well. In this, we see that the goal of anarchism is not only to put oneself in bondage while accepting the idea of freedom but eventually bringing about a Jesse James or Billy the Kid-type government. The fastest gets the property and the land. This is not what God had in mind. Anarchism is not God's tool of rule but rather the subjected will and an obedient spirit to His already established principles and laws.

Christians really need to wake up and understand that while we argue about the *isms* and *schisms* of our church doctrines, denominational differences, whether or not the Lord called a woman to preach, whose name we baptize in, and whether tongues is the sign and evidence of the Holy Ghost, other groups of anarchists are trying to steal the one thing that keeps us free; spiritual rule. We must never forget that all it would take to close the doors of all churches and institutions that entertain spirituality is one law.

Now that we have entered the 21st century, anarchism will become attractive to most people. There will still remain a remnant of God's people who will stay enslaved to the doings and will of the Lord. I emphasize the word *enslave* because we have been bought with a price (I Corinthians 6:20). Kropotkin wrote the first adept encyclopedia definition of anarchism in the eleventh edition of Encyclopedia Puritanical in the year 1910. The length of his definition does not impress its accuracy upon me. He introduces the word anarchism as the name given to a principle of theory of life and conduct under which society is conceived without government. Harmony in such a society is obtained not by submission to law and obedience to any authority, but by free agreements concluded between various groups. This tells us and shows us the trickery in anyone or anything that suggests that we become a society of anarchism.

When a name is given to a principle it does not substantiate a need for a government for the people. It mollifies the essence of the anointing. The anointing rules, it is the governor of our wholeness. When parts of our wholeness, such as the ability to define something we perceive and give definition to, starts ruling our society, it becomes clear to me how easy it is to think that we should operate without government. This also implies that we should do any and everything from an individualistic free standpoint. However, there is only one world, one God, one baptism and one true faith. People are coming up with many different varieties of everything. This is bound to result in warring chaos unless, of course, we embrace the anointing of God, that which expresses the essence of all that the Lord is. The anointing of the Lord can be felt, experienced and imparted from one to another. All of this is accomplished under rule and government. What a powerful tool!

I can only imagine what kind of government we could have if the United States of America would trust God's anointing to make decisions, and if all countries would do the same. (I guess it is alright to dream). We would then experience true peace. Instead, we are only experiencing peace talks, the breakdown of truths, etc. The devil wants us to believe that anarchism is misused and misunderstood by those who are spirit-filled. Anarchism does not impose a threat upon established government because the Lord God is in control. It is often a free ticket for a few people to control everything else. I do not know how we can separate anarchism from subtle communism. These definitions and explanations that I am trying to express are not frivolous and should not be taken as such. They are real. The spirit of anarchism is from the darkness of this world and suggests that the anointing of God be overlooked and disregarded. We must not forget that Jesus said that the thief would come to steal, kill and destroy

(St. John 10:10). Christ has already come that we may have life and that more abundantly.

I find it amusing that most pro-anarchists are still trying to blame capitalism so that they can hide behind their own subtle intent. It is the intent of anarchy to exclude the church as the ruling institution. Anarchism blames capitalism for drug abuse, gangs on TV and in movies, etc. Pro-anarchists suggest that if it were not for all of these binding laws then people would not be so hung up and paranoid about what the other person does thus bringing about a liberty which will automatically cause sin. Of course, they would not use the word *sin*. I sneaked that word in via my ecclesiastical instinct. Maybe they would use the word *chaos*.

A method used by anarchists to disregard the power and the authority of God's anointing upon our society is to draw a picture from their aspect of capitalism. To them, anarchy means keep the rich because they are leading everyone else. This is a true picture of what is happening because of the misuse of God's word, which is again, the governmental rule of laws and principles that we need for our society. When we misuse the Word of God we automatically put ourselves in bondage. The Word of God alone keeps and protects us from the influx of erroneous teachings. Thank God for the law! Thank God for government!

We really could talk forever on this subject but it may serve to give too much credit to the enemy's intent to sublimate our consciousness with interest and curiosity. I would rather suggest that we seek a closer walk with God. We should pray constantly that God will give us access to our personal portion of the anointing, the part of God that is in us, and that He will enable us to develop from this portion so that we may experience the victory that comes with being anointed.

David says in Psalm 23:5, "... thou anointest my head with oil...." Then he says, "...my cup runneth over." He goes on, "Surely goodness and mercy shall follow me all the days of my life: and I will dwell in the house of the Lord forever." What a wonderful phrase, "thou anointest my head with oil." Before David expressed his anointing, he talked about the Lord's benefits upon his life. He expressed the Lord's preparation of a table in the presence of his enemies, the Lord's rod and staff that constantly comforted him, and that he experienced evil attacks but he was not afraid because the Lord was with him. He had just come through the valley of the shadow of death and he still had his life. He talked about the Lord restoring him from falls and frailties. All of this came subsequent to the fact that the Lord had anointed his head with oil until his cup ran over. The Lord refilled him with the essence of all that He is. The Lord re-established his wholeness. That is what the anointing can do for us; re-establish our wholeness as it relates to our finances, physical health, and our mental and emotional stability. The Lord can restore all of this. He has given us an anointing. He has anointed us. We are His purposes. He created us, anointed us, and ordained us.

BOA is the acronym that I would like to use to indicate my commitment to this belief. It means that we are ***Blessed***, ***Ordained*** and ***Anointed.*** If we keep this concept in mind, which will always refresh our walk, we will constantly experience restoration even if we consider the parallel of anarchism and the misuse of government by capitalism. We still have the confidence with which we were blessed. We are ordained by the Lord, thus we are anointed.

There is a thin line between the anointing of the Lord and anarchy. One can see yet another intent in the spirit. It is to induce idolatry upon us and to help us remain in the state where we believe that we can do things without the Lord and maybe, He is not still on the throne. Let me say to all reading this book that God is still on the throne. He wants us to be encouraged, unconcerned about the yokes that are around our necks. Many times these yokes are not hindrances but our protection. If it were not for yokes, cattle would not stay within their proximity. They would roam and wander into other unprepared pastures thus making themselves vulnerable to the wild grass and the wild onions that could make them sick and eventually induce murrain. A yoke is not negative in this case. It serves as a protector.

I thank God for the times that He has allowed me to experience His easy yoke. Jesus says in St. Matthew 11:30, "For my yoke is easy, and my burden is light." My yoke is easy means it is bearable and durable. It is manageable. He will put nothing upon us that we are not able to handle. He will protect us, and many times in His protection it will seem as if He is putting us in bondage. His intent is to take the yoke from off our necks thus relieving the burden from off our shoulders (Isaiah 10:27). His intent is to keep us impressed with loving Him and to keep us impressed with the idea of Him being a Deliverer. It is easy for us to lose sight of the Lord as our deliverer. It would only take a carnal interpretation of our lives without godly intent and exclusive of spirituality, for us to believe that the Lord has become our enemy. This is the devil's strategy, which he has used in so many cases but the Lord is constantly anointing us with new knowledge and opening up revelations about our fulfillment from the inside of us.

This revelatory knowledge serves to protect us from all the intents of Satan. The Bible is filled with examples where the anointing fulfilled its purpose through acts of healing and deliverance. Isaiah made it very clear that the Spirit of the

Lord had anointed him. While many will give Jesus credit for this testimony, the record shows that Jesus was reading what Isaiah had said. Jesus was the anointing unless we want to say the anointing anointed Himself (consider Acts 10:38). Interpretation would have then been taken out of context. The anointing of God is an aid like medicine and a balm in Gilead. It anoints us with the oil of gladness and with joy that clothes us. It covers and protects us and becomes our hat. It is our outer shield against satanic attacks and at the same time it keeps our souls inside the perspectives of the Lord's design for our lives.

I John 2:27 lists abilities of the anointing. One such ability is to retrieve what God has given us. The anointing is a good teacher. It is the very thing that reminds us that He is the head of all principality and power (Colossians 2:10) and that we are the head and not the tail (Deuteronomy 28:13). It is the anointing that reminds us that contrition must be followed or accompanied with conviction. Consequently this will lead us to repentance, which will then give us restoration and reconciliation from the things we have done against the will of God for our lives. It is a sweet fragrance that stays with us and reminds us in the midst of stench, peril, and adversity, that we are greater than "he" that is against us. Romans 8:31 states, "What shall we say then to these things?" This is applicable if we are anointed. "If God be for us, who can be against us?"

I pray that our efforts will be to experience the anointing of God and not to fear the attacks of anarchism that has come upon the land. We should not worry about the inappropriateness of capitalism but rather trust the Lord to lead us and direct us with His anointing as our rule, as our principle, and as our law.

The enemy is upset with us and suggests that we change our government, our rule, and our belief in the Lord God. He also implies that we change the credence of the anointing and give it up. These are all insubordinate definitions. Christians should not practice these definitions. They should refuse to lower the standard of their conduct. It should be our behavior to trust in the Lord's anointing to remove yokes from our necks and burdens off our shoulders knowing that His burdens are light and His yokes are easy. We are impressed that God has given us a part, participation in this victorious walk of life. We fear no new unspiritual laws and governments. We know that these times are perilous but we are still powerful and we wish to project the promises of God not only in our lifestyles but also in our testimonies and professions. It is the anointing of the Lord God that destroys the yoke. The anointing maintains our intricate and intimate relationship with the Lord. In so doing, we can establish personal testimonies of the warmth, the love, the kindness, and the compassion of the God we serve. The Lord is available by accessing His anointing. He wants to anoint our hearts, our souls, and our minds.

Sometimes, it is taught that the anointing is only for a special group, a spiritual people. Everyone who is God's child has an anointing. This anointing must be developed. It knows its job if it is agitated through prayer and by studying the Word of God. It awaits the permission of the individual to rule and to become the governor. If we permit the Lord's anointing to govern our lives, it will lead us in the pathway of righteousness. It interprets God's Word and expresses God's feelings while imparting God's power upon our lives. It also gives us the wisdom, knowledge, and understanding to use this impartation to the glory of God. Our lives are designed to give God the glory and become the purposes of God that we may continue what we start and that we may fill the emptiness in the lives of others. The anointing of God gives us the knowledge that others need, and it always gives us the tongue of the learned that we might know how to speak a word in due season to those who are weary and out of the way (Isaiah 50:4).

In closing this chapter, I wish to state explicitly that society will be ruled by anarchy...the world will end. Although anarchy and its likes are seemingly growing, it is an indication to all Christians that this dispensation and this world are coming to an end. We should prepare our hallelujahs and praises because we are about to start using them throughout the day. We are about to experience the return of Jesus Christ.

CON-ARTISTRY AND SCAMS

This section is for educational purposes. See if any segment of it is relative to a church scheme you may have encountered.

DOG SCAM

For Entertainment and Understanding Value Only

Weil and Buckminster worked the pedigree dog swindle with alacrity for tens of thousands of dollars each year. Selecting a wealthy bar owner, Weil would saunter into a saloon, elegantly dressed and walking a finely groomed, richly scented dog that pranced at the end of an expensive-looking leash. Weil would tie the dog to the bar rail and then order a drink.

In the course of his conversation with the bar owner, Weil would proudly show pedigree papers for the hound along with several blue ribbon prizes the dog had won. He would then take out his solid gold watch and exclaim, "Great Scott! I'm late for an urgent business meeting!" He would then tell the bar owner, "I can't take Rex into the bank where I have my meeting. Will you be kind enough to watch my dog until my meeting is over?" Weil would slip a $10 bill on the bar, an unheard of tip, while cautioning the bar owner, "This dog is priceless so please watch him closely." He would then dash from the bar to keep his appointment.

A few minutes after Weil's departure, Fred Buckminster appeared in the bar. He stood next to the dog, ordered a drink, and then looked at the animal. He spat some beer in excitement and sputtered, "Oh, my Lord! I've been looking for this breed of dog for five years!" He quickly rummaged through his wallet and took out $50, shoving the money toward the bar owner, and begging him to sell him the dog.

"I cannot do that sir," came the usual response. "This dog belongs to a fellow who has left him only until his meeting is over. He'll be back in an hour."

"Okay, okay," Buckminster would say, "so you want more. Just say so. The animal is worth more. I'll make it $100!" He then placed $100 on the bar, offering the money to the owner.

"I told you sir, the animal is not mine to sell."

A half-hour elapsed before Weil reappeared. His demeanor had completely changed. He was no longer the confident, ebullient boulevardier. He was crestfallen as he slowly walked to the bar, almost oblivious of the dog.

"What's the matter, sir?" the solicitous bar owner asked. "You look like you've lost your best friend."

Weil shook his head sadly and then explained that his business deal had collapsed and that he was facing financial ruin. "I've been wiped out, emptied, nearly destroyed."

The bar owner seized the opportunity, offering to buy the dog for $200. Weil pretended to be in shock. "Sell Rex, the grand champion for only $200!"

After doing some quick mathematics, the bar owner invariably raised the offer by $25 to $50. He thought that since he already had Weil's $10 tip and Buckminster's $50 down payment, he would clear between $110 and $135 once the dog was delivered and Buckminster paid him the balance of the $250. Weil reluctantly took the purchase price from the bar owner while weeping, and then took his leave of the dog.

When the bar owner appeared, dog in hand, at the hotel where Buckminster was to be contacted, he quickly learned that no such person was registered there. Buckminster and Weil had pocketed between $165 and $190 for an investment of $60. They then returned to their own kennel, where street dogs or dogs from pounds were being groomed for the next sucker. On a good day, Weil and Buckminster could sell ten dogs, making as much as $5,000 a week.

THE HYPE, LAYING THE NOTE, RAISING CHANGE, ETC.

Definition

The hype is the process by which a cashier, bank teller or some other person is tricked into giving the con-artist more change than he should. It is also known as laying the note or raising change. It requires proper timing, knowledge of all the ins and outs of the con, and a small amount of cash.

How it works

There are many variations on how to operate the hype. The one presented here is the easiest version that I have come across and it is still very deceptive. It is best illustrated by an example.

Con man Friendly Frank walks into a coffee shop one rainy evening. Frank smiles at the cashier and comments on the miserable weather. The cashier states that she is not particularly fond of the weather of this city in general. Frank, while eyeing the pastries, orders a cup of coffee and a cinnamon roll to go. The cashier places the items on the counter and informs him that the total comes to $1.85.

Friendly Frank then pays her with a ten and she gives him one five, three ones, and fifteen cents for change. Frank adds the change to a pile of cash in his hand and comments to the cashier, "You know, I sure have a lot of ones here. Do you think you could give me back my ten for ten ones?" The cashier, who can always use more change, is happy to oblige. She pulls out Frank's ten, hands it to him, he gives her the ten ones and then begins to walk away. As the cashier counts the ones she finds nine ones and a ten dollar bill. She calls Frank back telling him that he has given her too much, that he gave her nine ones and a ten. Friendly Frank says, "I'm terribly sorry. I must have placed a ten instead of a one in there and given you a ten and nine ones. That makes nineteen dollars. Here, I'll give you another dollar. That makes an even twenty and you just take it all and give me a twenty-dollar bill. By the way, how do I get to the Italian restaurant from here?" She tells him it is just two blocks away while she puts away the twenty dollars and hands him a twenty-dollar bill. Friendly Frank thanks her for the directions and heads out ten dollars richer.

Did you catch that? The first time I read about this I said to myself, "I would have done just what the cashier did if I were her." It is easier to see what is wrong when in print than if it happened to you in real life. Sometimes, it is still hard to catch onto.

Basically the con man gives the cashier $20 in exchange for $30. The cashier gives Frank change twice for the ten ones. First, she gave him a ten for what she thinks is ten ones then she gives him a twenty. However, she had already given him a ten for ten of the twenty dollars she now has from him. We will count the first ten he gave her for the coffee, roll, and change as even since he wanted the coffee anyway. If you still do not see it, read through it a few times.

Points to consider

1. For this to work, Frank needs to get the ten before he gives her the nineteen dollars. If he does not get the ten first or at least trades simultaneously, the whole thing falls apart. This is the weakest part of the con, but it is also the key. So how does Frank help this happen?

> **a)** Frank says, "Can you give me my ten back," and points to it in the register.
> **b)** He moves down the counter, away from the cashier after he asks for his ten back.
> **c)** Frank takes his time counting out the ten ones (really nineteen).

2. He sure is not going to get too far after receiving the nineteen dollars. He makes sure to draw her attention to it if she has not counted or wants to pocket the extra herself. (Apparently, the cashier attempts to take advantage of this situation more often than you might think.)

3. Frank has the advantage since he knows what will happen before it happens. He understands this con inside and out. He knows what to say and it does not matter what the cashier does. Frank has seen all the variations of this script and thus has the upper hand.

4. One of the beauties of this short con is that it is almost impossible to get caught. Should the cashier catch on to the mistake Frank just professes his confusion (since it is rather confusing) and that he now sees the cashier is absolutely right.

5. Misdirection, timing, attitude, and clothing are all important to the successful completion of this con.

Frank knows just when to ask for directions to the restaurant. He has an easy friendly demeanor, yet speaks with authority (just take it all and give me a $20 bill). Frank is always well dressed because everybody knows that people who dress well are wealthy and should be treated with respect. Would a clean-cut guy like Friendly Frank try to cheat you? I think not!

The Con Artist

The clever con artist is a good actor who disarms his victim with an affable "nice guy" approach. Behind this friendly exterior is a shrewd psychologist who can isolate potential victims and break down their resistance to his proposals. Each conquest is part of a game in which he must "best" his fellow man.

The typical con-artist is amoral but seldom violent, and mobile with an excellent sense of timing. He sincerely believes his victims deserve their fate. If caught, he will probably strike again later. Con-artists are seldom rehabilitated.

The Victim

Anyone can be a victim, even a person who considers himself to be too intelligent or sophisticated to be "conned". During the 1920's, "Yellow Kid" Weil routinely swindled bankers saying, "That's where the money is." Many victims share certain characteristics. Often, but not always, they are older females who live alone. They are trusting of others, even strangers, and may need or desire supplemental income. Loneliness, a willingness to help, and a sense of charity are characteristics a con-artist will exploit to gain a victim's cooperation.

The con-artist ultimately will exploit his victim's assets including life insurance benefits, pensions, annuities, "nest eggs," home equity, or other tangible property. He will usually obtain the willing cooperation of his victim to complete the scheme.

Key words:

Cash only	Why is cash necessary for a proposed transaction? Why not checks?
Get Rich Quick	Any scheme should be carefully investigated.
Something for Nothing	A "retired" swindler once said that any time you are promised something for nothing, you usually get nothing.
Contests	Make sure they are not "come-ons" to draw you into a money-losing scheme.
Haste	Be wary of any pressure that you must act immediately or lose out.
Today Only	If something is worthwhile and available today, then it is likely to be available tomorrow.
Too Good To Be True	Such a scheme is probably not good or true.
Last Chance	If it is a chance worth taking, why is it offered on such short notice?
Leftover Material	Leftover material may also be stolen or defective.

Remember if it sounds too good to be true, it usually is!

- Never give your credit card number to a phone solicitor.
- Never purchase land that you have not seen.
- Never buy stock simply on the suggestion of a stranger.
- Never agree to home repairs that are quick, cheap or where you have to pay up front.
- Never send money as part of a chain letter.
- Always be alert. Swindlers and their scams usually cheat people out of nearly $40 million yearly! If you have been promised jubilee, please research it for yourself. You are going to be surprised.
- Be skeptical of things that simply sound too good to be true. If you are a victim of a con-artist, report it to God.
- Do not trust strangers who offer instant cash.
- Get more information before buying the "sure thing."
- Check charities before contributing.

THE "PIGEON DROP"

Strangers tell you they have found a large sum of money or valuables. They say they will split their good fortune with you if you put up some "good faith" money. You turn over the cash and you never see them or your money again.

THE "BANK EXAMINER" FRAUD

A so-called bank official asks you to help catch a "dishonest" teller by asking you to withdraw money from your account and turn it over to him or her. He or she can then do an audit or check the serial numbers. You do it and you never see the "bank official" or your money again.

THE "PYRAMID SCHEME"

Someone offers you a painless way to make money. You invest, and then you get others to invest, and they get others to invest and so on. Sometimes the initial investors are paid a small dividend to keep them happy. When the pyramid crashes, the only one with all the money is the one at the top and you cannot find him or her.

"WORK AT HOME" SCHEMES

You have seen the newspaper ads, "Great income for performing unskilled tasks at home!" Jobs like stuffing envelopes emphasize easy work, convenience and high hourly pay. Usually, after you pay for start-up supplies and a how-to book to get started, the market for your "service" usually dries up and you do not get your investment money back.

THE "FUNERAL CHASER"

Someone delivers a product to your door, like a Bible, that your deceased relative allegedly ordered before his or her death. You may even get a bill for an expensive item and you may be requested to make the final few payments. This scam artist uses the newspaper obituaries to prey on the bereaved families. You are not responsible for anyone else's purchases. If the claim is legitimate, the estate will settle.

Some rules:

-Always investigate before investing money or signing a contract.
-Be suspicious about extraordinary promises of high or unusual monetary returns, or a "bargain" no one else can match.
-Do not discuss your personal finances or give cash to strangers.
-Never be too embarrassed to report that you have been victimized or swindled.
-Testify in court if asked to help stop this kind of crime.

LORD LET ME DREAM

Lord let me dream
that I may envision my purpose.

Lord lend me your strength
that I may indulge in my purpose.

Then, grant me to be fervent
that I may fulfill my purpose.

For I realize that
at the conclusion of my purpose,

You will be fully and ultimately
glorified.

Apostle James S. Prothro